Welcom

Samsung Galaxy

The Complete Manual

Samsung's Galaxy range of Android devices continues to set the bar when it comes to mobile innovation. Whether it's the S7, S6 Edge+, Tab A or Note, each Galaxy combines superb hardware with a range of fantastic built-in software. In this revised edition of Samsung Galaxy The Complete Manual, we take you through everything you need to know to get the most from your Galaxy. From how to make use of your device's camera, to how to connect to an Android Wear device, read on to get started on your way to becoming a Galaxy expert.

Samsung Galaxy
The Complete Manual

Imagine Publishing Ltd
Richmond House
33 Richmond Hill
Bournemouth
Dorset BH2 6EZ
☎ +44 (0) 1202 586200
Website: www.imagine-publishing.co.uk
Twitter: @Books_Imagine
Facebook: www.facebook.com/ImagineBookazines

Publishing Director
Aaron Asadi

Head of Design
Ross Andrews

Editor in Chief
Jon White

Production Editor
Ross Hamilton

Senior Art Editor
Greg Whitaker

Assistant Designer
Sophie Ward

Photographer
James Sheppard

Printed by
William Gibbons, 26 Planetary Road, Willenhall, West Midlands, WV13 3XT

Distributed in the UK, Eire & the Rest of the World by
Marketforce, 5 Churchill Place, Canary Wharf, London, E14 5HU
Tel 0203 787 9060, www.marketforce.co.uk

Distributed in Australia by
Gordon & Gotch Australia Pty Ltd, 26 Rodborough Road, Frenchs Forest, NSW 2086, Australia
Tel +61 2 9972 8800, www.gordongotch.com.au

IMAGINE
PUBLISHING

Contents

What you can find inside the bookazine

Getting started

8 Introducing the Samsung Galaxy

14 Setting up your Samsung Galaxy

18 The first steps
Home screen and gestures

22 How to use your Samsung Galaxy

30 Applications
A guide to the native apps

The apps

 32 Settings, part 1
Network connections

 34 Settings, part 2
Personalise your Samsung Galaxy

 38 Settings, part 3
Change the device settings

 42 Android Wear
Connect to your Wear device

 44 Google Play
Download apps and media

 50 Galaxy Apps
Find discounts and collections

 54 Phone
Make a regular phone call

 58 Contacts
Store people's contact details

 62 Messaging
Send SMS and MMS messages

 66 Hangouts
Keep in touch with Google

 68 Email
Access multiple email accounts

 72 Internet
Browse the World Wide Web

 76 Camera
Take photos anywhere

 80 Gallery
View images and videos

 82 Story Album
Display your favourite photos

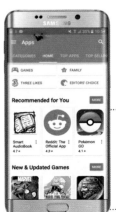

S7, S6 Edge+, Tab, Note, Alpha: there really is a Galaxy device for every Android user out there

Become a Galaxy master in minutes

 84 Kindle for Samsung
Read books

 88 Samsung Music
Listen to tunes on the go

 92 Video Player
Watch HD videos on your device

 96 Kids Mode
Tailor your device for kids

 98 Group Play
Play and share across devices

 102 Chromecast
Stream videos from your device

 104 Maps
Use turn-by-turn navigation

 108 Google Drive
Store your files on the cloud

 110 Google Now
Stay up to date with Google

 112 S Note
Write and draw notes by hand

 114 S Planner
Keep track of dates and tasks

 116 S Voice
Control apps with your voice

 118 S Health
Get fit and healthy

 122 S Translator
Converse abroad with your Galaxy

 124 Facebook
Update your status and more

 126 Twitter
Tweet wherever you are

Quickly access your favourite websites

Use your Galaxy to find your way around

Introducing the Samsung Galaxy

Just got a Samsung Galaxy device? Then discover how hard it can work on your behalf

Smartphones and tablets could be considered something of a beauty and the beast of the modern age. They are certainly beautiful to look at, many boasting sleek and stylish designs that are comfortable to hold and jaw-dropping in terms of design. And the sheer amount of functionality that is crammed into their compact units is nothing short of incredible. However, with such astounding wonder comes the beastly downside that we simply can't stop staring at them – they are just so distracting! If you read on, we'll outline exactly why you'll find it hard to put your Galaxy device down. Whether it's because of the look and feel of your smartphone or tablet, the intuitive operating system or the huge number of apps you can download and install, before too long you'll be hooked.

"We'll outline exactly why you'll find it hard to put your Galaxy device down"

Introducing the Samsung Galaxy

Hardware

Galaxy devices are versatile micro-computers that are capable of managing every aspect of your life – and there's a model to suit everyone. The Samsung Galaxy S7 is has taken over as the company's flagship device, boasting exquisite design, an ultra-responsive interface, an impeccably sharp display and lightning-quick charging to keep it all topped up. The S7, along with the S6 Edge, also runs the latest Android operating system, which crams even more functionality into your device. But while older models of Galaxy smartphones may be limited to the version of the Android OS they can run, they still boast a range of great features to make communicating and managing your life as effortless as possible.

If you prefer a bigger screen to work remotely or enjoy a film then the Galaxy Tab range is perfect. The dimensions of these devices vary, and include a 10.5-inch screen down to a smaller, but no less staggering 8.4-inch display. Finally there is the Galaxy Note range, which is geared towards working. The Galaxy Note Edge even has a curved screen, the 'edge' of which displays all of your notifications.

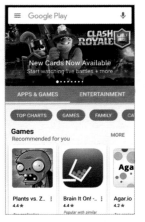

Fig 1 The Google Play Store is your first port of call for the latest and greatest apps

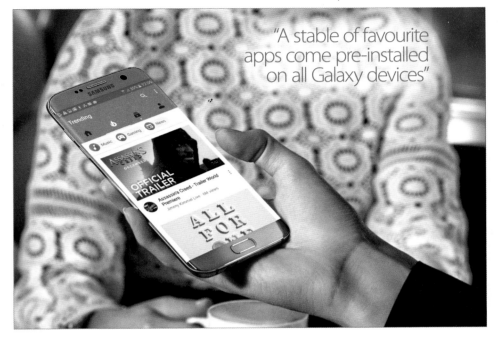

"A stable of favourite apps come pre-installed on all Galaxy devices"

OS/Apps

As we have already mentioned, Galaxy devices run on Google's Android operating system, which provides a wide range of apps and functions instantly. A stable of favourite apps that come pre-installed on your device include the Chrome web browser, Gmail, Maps and Google's media suite – Play Music, Play Movies & TV, Play Newsstand and Play Games. Then, of course, there is the Play Store app, which is your first port of call for all of the latest and greatest Android apps (as well as music, movies, books and games). Galaxy devices are also well provided for by Samsung too. TouchWiz is Samsung's own user interface that makes controlling Galaxy devices easier by providing shortcuts to your everyday tasks – and it is layered over the top of the Android interface with the two working in perfect unison. You will also find the Galaxy Apps service pre-installed on your Galaxy device, which provides instant access to Samsung's own app store. Though not as expansive or varied as the Google Play Store, this is still a great place to come for Galaxy-exclusive apps that may not come pre-installed on your device.

Fig 2 The Galaxy Apps store is the place to go for apps to get the most out of your Samsung device

☰ **My Drive**	Q ⠿ ⋮
Folders	Name ↑
📁 Football	📁 Holiday pics
📁 My files	📁 My Tracks
📁 Pet pics	📁 Projects

Fig 3 Google Drive comes pre-installed on your device and allows you to store your important files in the cloud

Getting started

Essential Galaxy downloads

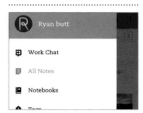

Evernote This brilliant app makes it hard to forget anything as you can create quick and easy typed, handwritten, voice or photo notes whenever you need to. Everything you create is synced and updated on all your devices.

Kindle Reading on your Galaxy has never been easier thanks to Kindle's online store, where you can download ebooks to read instantly, and a set of customisable display options.

BBC iPlayer With a decent Wi-Fi connection you can stream or download the latest BBC TV shows to enjoy when you want. This is just one of many quality streaming services available.

Introducing the Samsung Galaxy

Functions

As well as being infernal distractions, smartphones and tablets provide many positive uses to help you manage all aspects of your life. If you require your Galaxy device to work remotely then you'll find a wide range of apps available for word processing, creating and editing spreadsheets and putting together presentations – and everything can be saved and synced to select cloud computing apps, such as Drive and Dropbox, to ensure everyone concerned is working from the same document. If you just want to relax then you can, of course, use your device to play the latest movies downloaded or streamed from places such as Google Play Movies & TV and Netflix, or use it to enjoy a wide range of games, many of which give the specialist console devices a run for their money.

Your Galaxy device can also be used to keep fit and stay in shape. Not only are there apps to help you monitor your daily exercise and calorie intake, apps like YouTube also provide instant access to keep-fit videos. Whatever you need or want from your Galaxy device, you'll soon discover that, as the saying goes, "there's an app for that!"

Galaxy accessories

Wireless charging pad
If there is a curse of the modern mobile age then it is the amount of charging leads hanging out of our walls. This device lest you charge up your Galaxy devices simply by placing them on top.

Galaxy Note S Pen
This sleek and stylish stylus is designed for use with the Note 4 or Note Edge device, although it can also come in handy for navigating fiddly little smartphone keypads without removing your gloves.

Samsung Gear S2 Classic
This classic-looking watch gives you the freedom to enjoy a smart mobile experience without having to have your phone in hand. You can make and receive calls, check directions, monitor your fitness and more.

Galaxy Tab S Bluetooth Keyboard
The touch-screen interface has never been ideally suited to typing, but with a wireless keyboard such as this one you can touch-type with confidence that all of your button presses will be acknowledged.

LEVEL Box mini wireless speaker
As smartphones and tablets can be used to store all of your digital music and movie collections, investing in a wireless speaker to blast them out is definitely worth considering.

Book cover
As your Galaxy device is undoubtedly worth a lot of money, it makes good sense to protect it with a decent cover that can absorb the shocks and scratches that come as a result of dropping your device.

Setting up your Samsung Galaxy

The first few minutes you have with your Galaxy device will be spent setting it up. Invest time in this for an enjoyable and productive future

Setting up your Samsung Galaxy

1 Language When you take your new Samsung Galaxy device out of its box and have fully charged its battery, you will be ready to start using it. There is a setup procedure to go through first, however. Your first task is to tell your new Samsung what your language is. It should be set to English (United Kingdom) but you can tap the language bar to see more options if you need to change it.

2 Add Wi-Fi Next, select a Wi-Fi network. Your Galaxy device will then scan the surrounding area and show you all of the available networks that there are in the immediate vicinity. Depending on where you are, there could be quite a lot of them! You can identify your own network by its name – in order to log on, simply tap the name.

3 Enter password You will need to enter the password for your Wi-Fi network. Type this in using the keyboard – remember, you can long-press characters that sit on the top row of the keyboard to get to the numbers or just tap the bottom-left icon. Check Show password to double-check that you are entering it correctly, then select Connect when you are ready (Fig 1).

Fig 1 Enter your Wi-Fi access code

4 Connecting the Wi-Fi Having entered your password, wait for the next screen to appear. After a few seconds, you will see that you have been connected to your chosen Wi-Fi network. Even after doing this, all of the other networks that you could originally see will still be visible, meaning that it is easy for you to go back at any time and change networks.

5 Advanced options Tap on the Advanced option and you will then be able to set up some more Wi-Fi preferences, such as being notified when an open network is available and keeping Wi-Fi on when the handset is in sleep mode. You can also set up a timer to automatically connect to and disconnect from Wi-Fi networks on a regular basis (Fig 2).

Fig 2 Do more with your Wi-Fi

6 Set Wi-Fi timer If you turn the timer on with its slider button then tap the Wi-Fi timer text; you will go into a screen where you can set the starting and ending time for your Wi-Fi connection. This can be useful if, for example, you want to keep the handset on overnight, but save power by having Wi-Fi turned off. If you set this, tap Done at the top-right when you are finished (Fig 3).

When setting up your device you will be guided through the initial setup process to make life easier

Fig 3 Set up a sleep timer for your Wi-Fi

Getting started

Setting up your Samsung Galaxy

Fig 4 Create a Samsung account

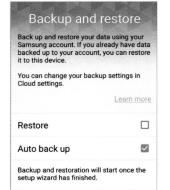

Fig 5 Add contact info to your account

Fig 6 Keep all your data safe

7 Date and time The next settings you change are for the date and time. You can set these manually or get your network to set them automatically. In most cases the latter will be perfectly fine. You can also select your time zone – although the network time settings should automatically do this for you. Regardless, you can always come and change this information later on.

8 Samsung Account Next, you can set up your Samsung account. Samsung lets you access a range of services, including Find My Mobile, which helps you locate a lost phone and even lock it so that if anyone else finds it they can't access your data. You can skip this and do it later if you like, but it is a good idea to do it sooner rather than later (Fig 4).

9 Create an account After agreeing to the terms and conditions of this account with a tap in the box that appears on the next screen and a tap of the Agree button, you are ready to set up your account. You will need to enter some details first, however, like an email address and password. Note down what you have chosen somewhere safe. You'll get an email to verify your account (Fig 5).

10 Backup and restore You can set up your Samsung account so that it will back up call logs, SMS and MMS messages, settings and other data (Fig 6). If you ever need to do a reset and have already made this backup beforehand, you can choose to restore the information to your Galaxy device when you come to this part of the installation process.

11 Google account Next, you will be asked to set up a Google account. You will need one of these to access Google Play and download apps. You'll get a Gmail email address as part of the process too, which gives you access to lots of useful stuff through the Google website. If you don't already have an account, answer No to 'Are you a Google user?' and then select Get an account.

12 Type in details Enter your real first and last names and then press the forward-facing arrow on the right side of the screen to move on to the next menu. There will be a short wait while your Galaxy device processes the information about your name. After this is finished, it will ask you to select an email address for your Google Mail address.

Your Samsung account can help you find a lost or stolen Galaxy, and can even be used to disable it

16

13 Try again You might find that the name you want to use has already been taken, and thus decide to try a new name instead. You can get Google to suggest some alternatives based on your first choice, or simply keep trying different choices until one that suits you appears by entering them and pressing Try again (Fig 7).

14 Password Next, you will need to enter a password for your Google account. When the option is made available, you will have to enter this twice in order to ensure that you have typed precisely what you want the first time round – make sure you choose something secure and memorable. After doing this, tap the forward-facing arrow on the right of the screen (Fig 8).

15 Security question Next, you need to enter a security question to help you recover your account if you ever lose your password. There are various choices on offer. Tap the down arrow by 'choose a security question' and then enter the answer. Add an email address to use for this process, too – not the Google Mail one you are creating.

16 Other Google services You can elect to join other Google services at this point – for example, Google Messenger and Circles – by joining Google+. Alternatively, you can choose to skip this step for now and complete it at a later date instead. If you decide to join now, all you need to do is select Join Now and the process will be complete (Fig 9).

17 Set your profile Your Google+ profile is set up with just your name to begin with. Next time you log in to Google+ you will be able to add more information to your profile, like a photo. For now, though, all you need to do is finish the setup, including turning on web history and entering an authentication code and your credit card details for Google Play.

18 Finishing off A final few screens finish off the process, including setting up the use of Google Location for location-based services and configuring a Dropbox account. Sign in now if you have an account, or wait and set an account up later if you prefer to do that instead. Then, all you have to do is tap Finish and you are good to go.

Google can use your location to help it deliver better and even more accurate information

Fig 7 Google can suggest names

Fig 8 Select a strong password

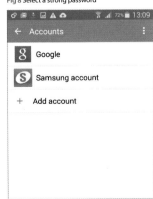

Fig 9 Join Google+ for more services

Learn the home screen

Here we show you around your Samsung Galaxy's home screen and notifications bar, then teach you the interaction gestures to use

Battery
Battery level is indicated here, and a lightning bolt icon shows if it is charging

Wi-Fi
You can see if you've got an active Wi-Fi connection by checking the tiny upload and download arrows just beneath the signal strength

Time
The time shows in the very top-right corner of the home screen

Common icons

Wi-Fi signal
This icon shows your Wi-Fi signal strength (the top bars) and whether the connection is active (the arrows)

3G/4G connection
Here you can see your mobile phone signal, its strength, and whether it is currently in operation

Missed call
You have a missed call. You can pull the notifications bar down to see more information and return the call

Battery (charging)
Your battery charge level is indicated and a white icon within shows if it is currently charging

Alarm
If you've got one or more alarms set then the alarm icon will be present in the notifications bar

Silent/vibrate
If you have your device set to silent or vibrate mode then an icon will show to indicate this

Blocking mode
Blocking mode stops you receiving unwanted calls and notifications. When it is activate you'll see this icon

Bluetooth
Bluetooth gives you access to short range wireless communications with other devices such as speakers

Downloads
When you are downloading apps and updates this icon will be displayed throughout the process

Google Play updates
When there are updates on Google Play this icon lets you know so that you can go and download them

USB connection
When your Galaxy device is connected to a PC via USB this icon will be shown in the notifications bar

GPS active
This icon shows you that the GPS function is active and currently locked onto your position

Dock
Put your favourite apps in the Dock and they'll be available on every home screen

Wallpaper
Wallpaper sits behind the icons. You can change this with a tap and hold of the home screen

Apps
Each application can be placed on a home screen and identified by its unique icon

Hand gestures on your Galaxy

There are many ways in which you can interact with your Galaxy's touchscreen interface…

1 Tap When you want something to happen with your Galaxy you generally have to touch the screen, and arguably the most basic of all the gestures is the tap (Fig 1). You tap to open an application, make a menu selection, activate a link in a web page, open an image or music track, and lots more too. Just press your finger down in the required spot and the device will recognise it.

2 Scroll When there's more information than you can see on a single screen, you have to scroll up and down to get to it. Hold a finger on the screen, move it vertically and the screen moves (Fig 2). You might scroll horizontally too – to move around image files or web pages, for example – but you will use the vertical scroll to glance through emails, settings screens, news feeds and more.

3 Swipe The swipe is a neat little gesture that's the counterpart of the scroll (Fig 3). We don't really call it a scroll, though, because devices like to use this gesture to quickly flick between adjacent screens, whether they're home screens on your device or pages inside an application. Just tap and slide to try it.

4 Drag (long-press) As well as tapping the screen to make things happen, you can also long-press. This means putting your finger on something and holding it down, and often allows you to drag your selected item around (Fig 4). You'll most likely use the long-press to move icons around, dragging them between different home screens or to the trash icon to remove them from home screens, or inside the app drawer to put them on home screens in the first place.

5 Pinch The pinch gesture is a really clever one. You'll use it to zoom out and make text or an image smaller. Simply put two fingers on the screen quite a way apart from each other when you have an image or web page showing on the screen, and then pull them towards each other to make what you are viewing smaller. Use it alongside the spread gesture for even more control.

6 Spread The spread gesture is best used with the pinch. Use it to zoom in and make text or an image larger. Put two fingers on the screen close to each other when there's an image or web page showing, then push them away from each other to make what you are viewing larger (Fig 5). Before you know it, the hand gestures that you use to operate your Galaxy will become second nature.

Fig 1 Simply tap the screen to select things

Fig 2 Tap and hold to scroll up and down

Fig 3 Pull your finger across the screen

Fig 4 Press and hold for a long-press

Fig 5 Reverse the pinch to zoom in

The first steps

Fig 1 Simply lift the handset to call

Smart gestures on your Galaxy

As well as having the standard Android gestures, Samsung Galaxy devices have a few of their own…

1 **Direct call** If a contact's details, such as their call log entry or a text message, are visible on the screen then the mere act of raising your Galaxy to your ear will be enough to call them. (Fig 1) You won't need to tap at the screen at all to identify them to the handset – it just knows what you want it to do. This makes calling a quick and easy process that requires minimum effort on your part.

Fig 2 Vibrations remind you of alerts

2 **Smart alert** Missing a call or message can be irritating, and you don't always glance at the screen to see the information that tells you something has been missed. You can use smart alerts to get your Galaxy to vibrate when you pick it up if there's a missed call or message, so that you know you need to check. This can be a life-saver if you happen to miss something important (Fig 2).

Fig 3 Quickly scale a long list

3 **Double tap to top** Sometimes you're working your way through a long list. Perhaps you're looking through your contacts to find someone, or rooting through old emails or reading a particularly long email message. Simply tap twice on the top of your Galaxy to go straight to the top of the list (Fig 3). This can save you seconds by enabling you to skip having to scroll back up again.

Fig 4 Bring the device in to zoom

4 **Tilt to zoom** Pinch to zoom is a well known Android gesture that's used on all handsets, but the Galaxy goes one better and lets you tilt the whole device to zoom. If you put two fingertips (or both thumbs) on the screen and tilt the handset away from you then it will zoom out of what's currently showing on the screen, and if you tilt it closer to you then it will zoom in (Fig 4).

Fig 5 Move apps around easily

5 **Pan to move icon** If you want to move icons to a different home screen, as a way of reorganising your shortcuts, you can drag one to the screen edge on any Android handset (Fig 5). With a Galaxy you can also hold the icon down with a fingertip and then pan your handset left and right to move it around (imagine the edge of your device is a hinge). It's a very cool system that works very well.

6 **Pan to browse images** If you are currently viewing a large image on your device that runs over the edges of the visible screen area, you may want to pan around to see more of it. To do this, you can simply hold a fingertip on the screen and then move the entire handset up, down, left and right to pan around the image, as though you were holding a window onto it.

Motions and gestures

Air browse
On

Direct call
On

Smart alert

Use the Motion settings on your device to turn these different gestures and settings on and off

Fig 6 Refresh with a wrist-flick

7 Shake to update There are lots of apps that update their content regularly. Email, news apps and the Samsung weather widget are a few examples. You can force updates of these apps by interacting with the refresh buttons, but the Galaxy also lets you update by just shaking it (Fig 6). No finger prodding necessary here, just shake the device to stay up to date with the latest apps.

Fig 7 Flip for silence

8 Turn over to mute/pause Sometimes an incoming call comes along just at the wrong time, or an alarm sounds and it is inconvenient. You might want the simplest possible way of silencing these intrusions, or of shutting off music playback for a while. Well, the simplest way is to turn your Galaxy face down (Fig 7). That's right, just flip it over to mute all unwelcome distractions.

9 Palm swipe to capture screen There is a key combination that lets you save an image of whatever your device is currently displaying – hold down the Power and Home buttons together. However, you can also do it by sweeping the edge of your hand from one side of your Galaxy to the other (Fig 8). It's neater, faster and is far easier than using any button combinations.

Fig 8 Take screenshots in seconds

10 Palm touch to mute/pause If you are watching a video or listening to music and you want it to just stop for a few minutes, you could pick your Galaxy up and hit the pause button. There's a simple gesture that can do the job too, though. If you put your whole palm on the screen, your device will be silenced (Fig 9). Ideal for when you don't want to be disturbed.

Fig 9 Cover it up to mute or pause

11 Smart scroll (S5/S4 only) If you want to work your way through an email or a document and don't fancy using the basic finger gestures to scroll, then you can achieve the same thing by just tilting your Galaxy S5/S4 back and forth and letting the page slide up and down. It's an immersive way to browse through your content, but the feature was discarded for the S6 onwards.

12 Air gesture (S5/S4 only) You don't even have to touch the Galaxy S5/S4 in order to use gestures. The new Air Gesture controls allow owners of this flagship device to wave their hand in front of their screen to skip between music tracks or queued videos, answer incoming calls and more (Fig 10). It's handset control with the very lightest of touches.

Fig 10 Wave your hand to control

How to use your Galaxy

Now you know how to interact with your device, it's time to start using it

When you get your new Galaxy up and running you're going to want to start making the most of it right away. There are a few tips about using the hardware and the software that will get you off to a running start.

One of the great things about the Galaxy is how easy it is to access key features and work with apps. Here we're going to run through a few things that will help you get started and use some of the main functions like Wi-Fi and GPS, as well as how to start customising the layout of your home screens.

"One of the great things about the Galaxy is how easy it is to access features and apps"

Switch your device on and off

2 Power options Hold the button down to see more power options.

1 Switch on The on/off button will most likely be on the top or the right long edge of your device. Give it a gentle press to switch your Galaxy on. If you aren't using it for long periods of time then you might consider turning it off again.

3 Power off Simply tap Power off at the top of the list to shut down.

Restart or lock your device

1 Restart your Galaxy Hold the power button down for a second. Select Restart from the power options to reboot your device.

2 Lock your Galaxy Give the power button a quick press to turn the screen off and lock your Galaxy.

Recharge your Galaxy device

2 Adaptor Put the other end into the adaptor that came with your Galaxy.

1 Charging up Your Galaxy is charged via Micro USB. The charge port will probably be on the bottom edge, though it might be on one of the sides. Grab your Micro USB cable and insert the smaller end into the charge port.

3 Computers You can charge up by plugging into a computer instead.

Change the volume

2 Volume in apps Some apps also have an on-screen volume slider.

1 The volume keys You can change the volume of audio on your Galaxy using the Volume 'rocker' button that's usually found on the left long edge. Pressing the top end raises the volume while pressing the bottom end lowers it.

3 Earphone controls You can also use your Samsung earphones' controls.

Using the notifications area

Quick settings
Icons at the top of the screen let you make quick adjustments to the settings and feature

Find things
Tap on S Finder and tap in keywords to quickly find things stored on your Galaxy device

Third-party apps
Some apps you install on your device, such as Dropbox, will also use the notifications area

Reveal the area
To see your notifications area in full, drag the top bar (containing the time) down from any screen

Tile icon
To display all quick settings tap the top-right tile icon. Tap on the buttons to access the apps or turn on or off

Screen brightness
You can manually adjust the brightness of the screen here or tap Auto

Access the Settings toggles

1 Quick access Drag the notifications bar down to see the whole area.

2 Tap to use Tap on buttons such as Wi-Fi and GPS to turn them on or off.

3 More settings Swipe to the left to see even more settings toggles.

Organise apps with folders

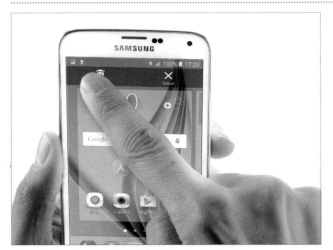

2 Name it You'll be asked to give the new folder a name, so type away.

1 Drag the app You can put apps into folders by dragging them onto the Create Folder icon that appears at the top of screen when you 'pick one up', or onto existing folders. This will help you to keep your home screens nice and tidy.

3 Change it Tap a folder to open it, and tap on its name to change it.

Customise the dock

1 Drag out of the dock
Tap and hold an app in your dock and then drag it up to Remove.

2 Drag into the dock
Choose an app on your home screen and drag it into the dock.

Inside the App Drawer

Adding widgets
Press and hold on a home screen to bring up options to add widgets relating to your apps

Menu options
Tap here to create folders, uninstall/disable apps and much more

All the apps
All the apps installed on your device can be found here

Navigation
You can use these dots to quickly move between App Drawer pages

Open the Drawer
To get here, just tap the Apps icon in your Dock

Add apps to home screens

1 **Find your app** Go to the app drawer and locate the app you want.

2 **Select it** Tap and hold the app and it'll overlay onto the home screen.

3 **Drop it** Now just take your finger off the app to drop it into place.

Multitasking on your device

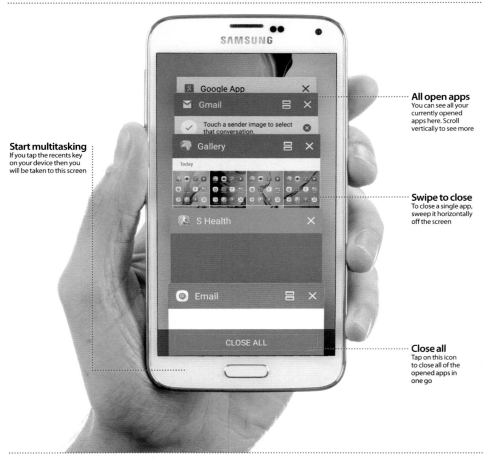

Start multitasking
If you tap the recents key on your device then you will be taken to this screen

All open apps
You can see all your currently opened apps here. Scroll vertically to see more

Swipe to close
To close a single app, sweep it horizontally off the screen

Close all
Tap on this icon to close all of the opened apps in one go

1 Task manager Tap on the chart icon in the lower-left corner (if available).

2 End all apps Hit the End All button to deactivate all running apps.

3 Clear apps Tap the right-hand icon to instantly clear all active apps.

Share your content

2 Where to share Tap the icon and then choose the app to share with.

1 Share files If you have files such as images or audio that you would like to share with other people, you can tap the share icon that appears whenever it can be used. The icon, shown above, looks like a little 'less than' mathematical symbol.

3 Attach and share Follow the required procedure method.

Search using Google

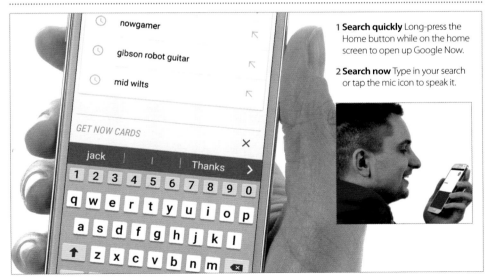

1 Search quickly Long-press the Home button while on the home screen to open up Google Now.

2 Search now Type in your search or tap the mic icon to speak it.

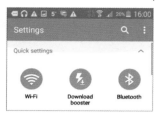
Fig 1 Control your Galaxy device

Fig 2 Discover apps and discounts

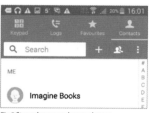
Fig 3 Store phone numbers and more

Fig 4 Start browsing the web

Fig 5 Take photos wherever you are

Applications

These are the key applications that you will be using every day with your Samsung Galaxy device

Settings The Settings area, accessible via its app icon or by pressing the Menu button from the home screen and selecting Settings, allows you to control every aspect of your device.

Play Store Google Play is the main hub for content on your Samsung Galaxy device. Here you can browse, download and share apps, games, movies, music, books and magazines.

Galaxy Apps Galaxy Apps is a portal to apps and games that offers many discounts and deals as well as a fresh system of categories, including apps selected by Samsung and featured collections.

Phone The mainstay of mobile devices, your Samsung Galaxy also has its cornerstone Phone app. You can dial directly using the keypad or start typing names to find your saved contacts.

Contacts The Contacts app is a powerful tool that amalgamates your contacts data saved in a range of places, including Google, Facebook and LinkedIn, and provides quick access to calls and messages.

Messages Messages allows you to keep in touch with everyone important to you. You can send SMS or MMS messages, and make calls by simply lifting your phone during a text conversation.

Hangouts Google's new messaging service neatly wraps its predecessors into a neat, functional app that lets you carry on the conversation you're having in your Circles on your Galaxy device.

Email Samsung's Email app is a useful tool for managing multiple email accounts, allowing you to direct all your mail to one handy app with full search, folder and labelling capabilities.

Internet The Internet app is your first port of call when it comes to surfing the web. Browsing is fast and simple, and you can zoom out to the tab view by simply pinching.

Camera The Camera app is a very versatile tool that provides you with a deluge of options ranging from fun filters to pro photographers' settings, and it also has a number of handy launch shortcuts.

Gallery All the photos you take, as well as the screenshots you save, the images you download and those you transfer from other devices, can all be viewed from within the Gallery app.

Applications

Getting started

Fig 6 Listen to your favourite tunes

 Story Album Import your images from the Gallery app into customisable photo albums using Story Album. You can apply themes, add captions and text, and share and print your albums.

 Samsung Music You can play all your tunes from within the Samsung Music app or by adding its widget to your home screen. You can also import more tracks quickly and easily.

 Video Player Supporting subtitles and a range of file formats, Video Player is your Samsung Galaxy's main viewing screen. You can browse the files on your device, queue videos up and hit play.

Fig 7 Get personalised fitness advice

 Smart Remote This versatile app not only transforms your Galaxy device into a remote control for your TV and set-top box, but it also sources and recommends shows to watch.

 Group Play This app lets you pair-up multiple devices and share pictures, documents and music among them in real-time. You can also download and play multiplayer games through the interface.

Fig 8 Access turn-by-turn directions

 Group Camcorder A new expansion of Group Play, this allows you, as director, to view all camera feeds in the group and then edit and merge them into the best shot sequence.

 S Health This app helps you manage your health as well as lets you set fitness goals, check your progress and keep track of your overall health. Create a profile and monitor your diet and exercise.

 Google Drive An incredibly useful tool for backing things up, as well as sharing photos, documents and other files across devices, Google Drive offers users plenty of free storage online.

Fig 9 Sketch out your reminders

 Clock Use this handy app to set yourself alarms, see what time it is in other places around the world and get instant access to a stopwatch to record laps and a timer to assist you in the kitchen.

 Maps Google's Maps app shows you what's going on nearby, places to eat, drink and more. Plus, with turn-by-turn navigation for in-car or in-pocket setups, you'll never get lost again.

 S Note Whether you're using your finger or the S Pen, you can jot all your important notes down for later using the S Note app (or its sibling, S Memo) and even link them with your S Planner tasks.

 S Planner S Planner is both a comprehensive calendar, pulling in data from your Google and Facebook calendars, and an organiser that you can use to set reminders, manage to-do lists and more.

 S Voice S Voice can be used to find information by asking questions and also to control your device's apps and settings. With a voice activation command to wake up S Voice, you need never touch your device again.

Fig 10 Manage your schedule effortlessly

Settings – Network connections

You'll use it to...

Get online
Surf the web

Distribute music
Share tracks between devices

Pass on pictures
Share photos between devices

Personalise your device
Change the ringtone and more

Create a hotspot
Share the Internet between devices

Update your status
Tweet your thoughts

Get entertainment
Use download and streaming services like
the BBC iPlayer

Use Wi-Fi and the mobile phone network to get in
contact with the world

Introducing Settings

Settings is where you can
configure a wide range of
different aspects of your
device to get them just how
you like them, personalising
the look and feel, responses
to gestures and a lot more.
Settings is also where
you configure wireless
connections and networks.

Fig 1 (right) On the home page, select your
App Drawer. Scroll to find Settings. Tap it
and you will be inside the settings area

Fig 2 (above) Find a Wi-Fi network and
connect to it via Settings

Connect to Wi-Fi

When it comes to Wi-Fi,
getting connected is really
easy. First you need to
make your way to the Wi-Fi
settings area on your Galaxy
(Fig 1). Then use the slider
to turn Wi-Fi on. This screen

also lists all of the Wi-Fi connections your Galaxy can find (Fig 2).
Tap one, enter its password and then tap Connect. Your Galaxy
will remember networks it has connected to in the past, so there's
no need to keep entering the passcode every time you want to
connect. Better yet, it will automatically connect whenever you
come into the vicinity of a network you've used before, so moving

Settings – Network connections

The apps

off your data connection and onto your home Wi-Fi is seamless. This will matter a lot if your network data allowance is low.

Wi-Fi passwords can be a complex mix of letters and numbers, and it can be tricky to enter them correctly. If you find your Galaxy won't connect, maybe you are entering the information incorrectly. Just choose Show password if you find you are having a problem and double-check what you are entering as the passwords

Share via S Beam

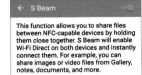

This function allows you to share files between NFC-capable devices by holding them close together. S Beam will enable Wi-Fi Direct on both devices and instantly connect them. For example, you can share images or video files from Gallery, notes, documents, and more.

Simply bring the devices together, back to back, then tap your screen. The

Create a Wi-Fi hotspot

If you have a Wi-Fi-only device you want to connect to the internet when you're out and about, like a laptop, you can do so via your Galaxy. Simply create a Wi-Fi 'hotspot' using your Galaxy and then connect to it with the Wi-Fi-only device.

In Settings, under Network Connections, tap on Tethering and Wi-Fi Hotspot. Use the slider to turn Portable Wi-Fi hotspot on, then make a note of the password and use it in your other device to connect.

1 **Use S Beam** Share files between Galaxy devices by using Near Field Communication (NFC).

2 **Find S Beam** Go to Settings and under the Connect and Share, settings, tap the NFC option.

Tethering via Bluetooth

As well as using Wi-Fi to allow other devices to share your Galaxy's internet connection, you can also use Bluetooth in the same way. The setting is similar to using Wi-Fi.

To get the Bluetooth method to work, go to Settings and tap on the Tethering and Wi-Fi Hotspot option under Network Connections. Next you need to tick the box next to Bluetooth Tethering. This will turn Bluetooth on and any device that's paired with your Galaxy will be able to get to the internet through the connection – pretty impressive.

3 **Turn on** Tap S Beam and use the slider to turn S Beam on, then hit the Back button.

For open Wi-Fi network alerts, under Wi-Fi, tap on the menu icon and choose Advanced

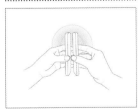

4 **Transfer** Activate S Beam on the other device, hold the two back-to-back and tap when told.

Settings – Personalisation

Change your Galaxy to suit your tastes

You'll use it to…

Change the font
Make your menus more readable

Set your lock screen
Customise the available options

Pick ringtones
Give your friends bespoke alerts

Prevent cold calls
Block unwanted callers

Save battery
Set up Power saving mode

Choose wallpapers
Change your device's background

Fig 1 (right) You can personalise your Galaxy device in a number of ways

Fig 2 (above) You can make precise changes to the vibration intensity for different circumstances

Customising your Galaxy device

When you first set up your Galaxy device, many settings will have been taken care of. There's a lot you can do to personalise these, though, from changing the home and lock-screen wallpapers to altering the fonts or the sounds used for ringtones, alerts and more. Different Galaxy devices have different features – here, we're looking at the Galaxy S7 (Fig 1).

Control the system sounds

There are lots of different ways in which your Galaxy device uses sound. The one that is likely to spring to mind immediately is ringtones, but there are many others. How about all the different kinds of notifications for different incoming communications? There are lots and lots of built-in sounds that you can use as ringtones and notification alerts, and experimenting with them can be an entertaining experience.

In fact, some of the sounds aren't really like noises at all. These relate to vibrations and something called 'haptic feedback', which refers to those small tactile jolts you get when you tap and hold app icons on the screen. There is a sound associated with these, but it's really much more about vibration – as is full vibration, of course, which you can use for an alert if you want to turn the ringtone volume off. You can even make changes to that in order to make it stronger or weaker in different circumstances (Fig 2).

Customise the display

Personalising the look of your Galaxy device is a great way to make it truly yours, and there are lots of features that enable you to do this. For example, if you tap Settings and go to Display, you will see lots of choices. You can change the display font and alter how the LED indicator is used – by setting it to flash red if the battery gets low, for instance. You can also use the Smart Stay function whereby the front camera is used to keep the screen on if you are looking at the device, which instantly eradicates any frustration when the screen dims and locks when you leave it idle for a few seconds.

Adjust the screen settings

The screen is the most power-hungry part of your device, so you'll want to ensure it works to a sufficiently high standard but, at the same time, doesn't consume power at an unnecessarily fast rate. There are some key options to help you get the best out of your device, and you'll find them in the Display part of the Settings app.

Here, you can manually alter the screen brightness or set it to automatically adapt. Moreover, you can set the screen to time out after a period of inactivity – on the Galaxy S7 this ranges between 15 seconds and ten minutes. You can also use Smart Stay to keep the screen on while you are looking at it.

You can alter the screen brightness, choosing to adjust it either manually or automatically

Set ringtones and alerts

1 Go to settings Tap Settings and then Sound to get to the sound settings area.

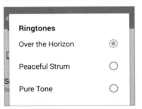

2 Select a ringtone Tap Device ringtone, then tap the tones to test them and hit OK to set one.

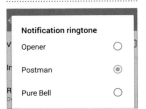

3 Alerts Tap Default Notifications to go to the notifications area, tap to test and hit OK to select.

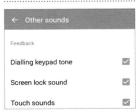

4 Vibrate when ringing If you want your Galaxy device to vibrate, just tick the box.

Settings – Personalisation

Change the lock screen

The lock screen isn't just a screen that appears when your handset has timed out; it can also provide you with some very useful functions. On the Galaxy S7, you can set it to display lots of different kinds of information, including a clock, weather data and a rolling 'ticker' of information from sources like Facebook.

The lock screen can open directly into five different applications – what they are is up to you (Fig 3). This is one of the best shortcuts you can set up. If you frequently pick up your Galaxy device to make a phone call, check your email, tweet, take a photo and so on, the chances are that you can put a shortcut to the relevant app on the lock screen and get there in an instant.

Fig 3 (above) You can set apps to open directly from the lock screen

Shortcuts
Go to Toolbox to create a shortcut to apps

Clock
Add a clock icon by selecting this option

Owner info
Add your own user info to the lock screen

More info
Tap here to display the weather and a pedometer

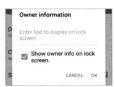

Add your owner details to the lock screen in case your missing device is found by someone

To get started with this feature, tap on Toolbox under the Sound and Display settings and then move the Toolbox slider to the On position. This will illuminate the default applications but you can change these by tapping on Edit and then deselecting existing apps before choosing new ones.

Set up Blocking mode

Most of the calls and texts we get are generally from people that we actually want to hear from. However, as you will probably appreciate by now, that's not always the case since we occasionally, and for any number of reasons, receive unwelcome phone calls from people that we just don't want to hear from. You will be happy to hear that you can block incoming phone numbers to make sure that you don't have to take their calls. Go to the Call settings and then tap on 'Call Rejection'. Now select the Auto reject list and then tap on the '+' icon to add new numbers to block. You can also block callers form within the Phone app by tapping on the number and then tapping the three-dot icon in the top-right corner and selecting the 'Add to Auto reject list' option from the menu. You can always remove numbers later if you wish.

Block calls

1 Find the Call settings Tap Call and then choose Call rejection>Auto reject list.

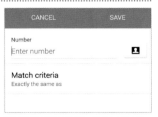

2 Enter numbers Now tap on the '+' icon and type in the number that you wish to block.

Enable Power saving

1 Power saving Head over to the Settings menu and slide on the Power saving mode.

2 More settings Tap Power saving mode in order to get to more detailed options.

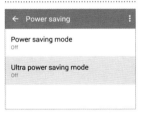

3 Ultra power saving mode For more extreme power-saving methods, tap this option.

4 Drastic cutbacks This mode greyscales the screen and limits which apps you can access.

Settings – Device

Understand how to make Settings work for you

You'll use it to...

Set passcodes
Protect your Galaxy device

Update firmware
Make sure you have the latest OS

Check your number
Find your phone number

Simplify the device
Use the accessibility settings

Manage space
Check on your device's storage

Remove apps
Uninstall unwanted apps

Managing your Samsung device

Your Samsung Galaxy device will work right out of the box, but using it will be a more fun experience if you personalise its settings to meet your own requirements. This is easy to do, and the Settings area has a lot on offer (Fig 1). What you get will vary from device to device, but it's all logically arranged and all of the settings are handily placed into easy-to-find sections.

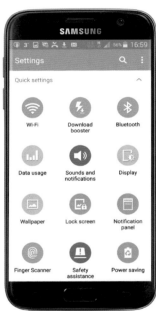

Fig 1 (right) The Settings area can be complex but it is logically arranged

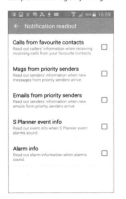

Fig 2 (above) You can set up Notification readout mode on your device

Change the language settings

When you set your Samsung Galaxy device up for the first time, you need to tell it your preferred language. However, there's more to the language settings area than just telling your Galaxy what language it should use as its main one; you can also set up a range of other language and speech-related preferences. If you go to the Settings area of your Galaxy device and tap Language and input, you will have access to these settings.

So for example, you are able to change how voice search works by setting a default language and then asking it to block offensive words. Moreover, you are also able to set some text-to-speech options. You can also decide how fast speech synthesis runs, setting

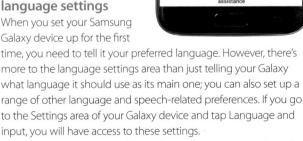

it to talk at different speeds depending on what your preference might be.

There's also a really useful Notification readout mode (Fig 2). This enables you to set incoming calls and new notifications to be read out automatically. You can decide precisely what gets read out, and in the process avoid getting overwhelmed.

Finger Scanner

One of the hottest features of the Galaxy S6 is the Finger Scanner, which is used as an alternative to entering passwords. This technology sits within the home button on your device and Samsung has already made this feature available to third-party developers to integrate into separate apps (the PayPal app is the first to utilise the Finger Scanner for added security).

Setting up the Finger Scanner is quick and easy, and can be done in the Finger Scanner option in Settings (under Quick Settings). You'll need to slowly swipe your finger down over your home button a number of times to register your fingerprint and then provide an alternative password as a back-up option. Once your print has been registered you will be taken to the Lock screen settings so that you can set it as a high-security means of unlocking your device.

Use the accessibility options

To discover ways in which you can make your Galaxy device easier to use, tap on the Accessibility heading in Settings. This area groups together a lot of different options that you might find useful if you have a disability or would just like a bit of help with certain things. For example, you can change the font size that's used across the device, and reverse the screen colours to make it easier for you to read. You can also change the sounds from stereo to mono and set up a front light for notifications. There are even settings for the tap-and-hold time and much more besides.

If you forget your phone number, you can find it by heading to Settings> About Device>Status

Set up Finger Scanner

1 Quick Settings Open Settings and tap 'Finger Scanner' listed under Quick Settings.

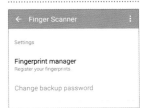

2 Fingerprint manager Tap on the Fingerprint manager option and then tap OK.

3 Register print Now slowly swipe your finger down over the home button multiple times.

4 Screen lock You will then be taken to the Lock screen settings where you can select it.

Settings – Device

Fig 3 Check the storage space on your device and microSD card

Check storage space

Your Samsung Galaxy has a set amount of space for storage, and once that is full you will find that you can't cram anything else onto it unless you remove something to save space. Fortunately, most smartphones and tablets let you add to the built-in storage space using microSD cards, and the Samsung Galaxy S7 has that feature. With cards available offering storage of up to 128GB, you can add lots more storage space to your Galaxy, and that space can accommodate both apps and data (including music, movies and much more).

It is easy to check the amount of storage space that's available on your Galaxy. Simply head over to the Settings area and then scroll down to Storage. Tap on that and you will be able to see how much

Pattern recognition
Pattern recognition is easy to use, and offers reasonably good security

PIN
An old-fashioned PIN offers good protection

Password
Your phone is most secure with a password that uses a combination of letters and numbers

Fingerprint
You can scan your fingerprint using the home button for a higher level of security

Think about how secure the different lock systems are. A password offers the highest level of security

device memory is being used by different types of media. You can also check the amount of storage that is free on your microSD card, unmount the card so that you can remove it safely, and even format it (wipe all the data off it).

Use the security settings

After you've owned a Samsung Galaxy for a little while, you will find that it will have all sorts of personal information stored on it. This could include contact details, Facebook logins, logins for a range of other apps, web-based services and more. However, you will need to be careful, as these services could be used to give people access to personal information like your bank account or other important data that you don't want others to see.

In order to protect your personal data, always log out of web services when you're done with them and take advantage of the numerous security features that are available on your Samsung Galaxy device. There are several options available, including the remote Find My Mobile service that enables you to locate and even wipe your Galaxy device from a distance, and you can also set up your device to use PINs and logins for added protection.

Lock your screen

1 Screen lock options In the Settings menu, tap Lock Screen followed by Screen Lock to see the options.

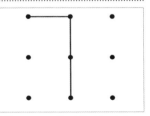

2 Choose a method Decide what kind of method you want to use and then tap on it to set it up.

Update your firmware

1 Firmware update You can check to find out if there's an update waiting. Tap Settings.

2 About Device Tap About Device in order to progress to the next screen.

3 Software update Tap Software Update and then set your preferences for checking.

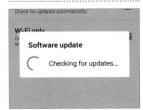

4 Check for updates Tap Update and then follow through to check for updates.

Android Wear

Get all of your Galaxy's notifications sent to your smartwatch – even when you leave it at home

You'll use it to...

Receive messages
View your messages and app notifications with a flick of your wrist

Set reminders
Dictate reminders to the watch and receive alerts about your appointments

Check the weather
Glance the weather forecast for the day ahead when wake up in the morning

Track your fitness
Keep track of your activity and get updates about your step count and heart rate

Play music offline
Store your favourite songs to your watch for when your Galaxy's not around

Get directions
Provided your watch and Galaxy have Wi-Fi, get turn-by-turn navigation to places

Fig 1 (below) To give your smartwatch internet access, install the free Android Wear app from the Google Play Store

Fig 2 (right) View all of your Galaxy's updates on your wrist, so you can respond to messages and notifications more easily

View your Galaxy on your wrist

Smartwatches are all the rage right now, so you'll be glad to hear there are lots of models that work with your Galaxy device.

The most popular smartwatches run a system called Android Wear. These come in a wide variety of designs, with a choice of circular or square watch faces and different watch straps, but all work similar to your Galaxy's Google Now assistant.

When set up, messages and notifications from your device will be sent to the watch as easy-to-understand information cards. Read on to find out more about how your Wear works in conjunction with your Samsung Galaxy.

Get the companion app

However, Android Wear watches can't access Wi-Fi in the conventional manner, so without connecting it to your device, your smartwatch can't do much more than a digital watch. To set up this connection, you will need to install the Android Wear app on your device. From within this app, you can then connect your Galaxy with your smartwatch via Bluetooth. Once this connection is set up,

all of your Galaxy's notifications will be redirected to your smartwatch. Newer Android Wear models can then work independently of your device, relaying messages and more, as long as your smartwatch and smartphone or tablet are connected to Wi-Fi networks, no matter the distance.

View Google Now cards

As well as displaying all the messages and notifications sent to your device, your smartwatch will display useful information from Google Now in the form of simple cards. These can include reminders to leave on time for an upcoming appointment, sports scores for your favourite team and traffic alerts for your journey home. You can slide up and down your watch screen to view various cards, or swipe the card from right to left to see more information, such as view a weather forecast for the next few days, or open the information on your Galaxy. Once you're done with a card, you can swipe left to dismiss it.

Track your health

As well as getting essential updates, the other advantage to using Android Wear is being able to track your health. With a built-in Google Fit app, every smartwatch can quietly count your footsteps while you wear it, and some models also measure your heart rate. You can then view this data as a short graph on your watch, or in detail on your Galaxy. If you're using a Samsung Gear Live smartwatch, this will relay fitness data directly to your Galaxy's S Health app instead. Some Android Wear watches have GPS sensors, so they can also log your route when you go jogging.

To get a guided tour of your Android Wear device's features, open menu options and select the Tutorial option in the smartphone/tablet app

Pair your smartwatch

1 Download Android Wear app
Install the app from Google Play store and open it on your device.

2 Pair devices via Bluetooth
Select 'Pair with a new wearable' from the drop-down menu.

3 Confirm pairing To confirm step up tap the tick mark on watch and press OK on screen.

4 Receive notifications Go to Notification Settings in the app to allow the watch to update.

Google Play

Google Play

Get more content onto your Galaxy device by using the Google Play store

You'll use it to…

Download apps
Add paid and free apps to your device

Rent movies
Watch the latest blockbuster films

Subscribe to magazines
Get digital copies of your favourite magazines delivered instantly

Stream music
Listen to the latest tracks and albums

Read books
Download books from a range of genres

Update your content
Manually update your apps and other assorted media

Fig 1 (right) The Play Store's home screen features links to all the different sections

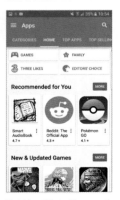

Fig 2 (above) Most paid apps need a one-off payment before you can install them

Introducing Google Play

Google Play is constantly expanding with new content on a daily basis. As well as offering over 850,000 apps and games, users can now find dedicated music, movies, books and magazine sections that are filled with even more content than ever (Fig 1).

Purchasing apps

With over 1 million apps at your disposal, you're never going to run out of new content to fill up your device. What you'll notice about some apps is that they're free to download, while the rest require you to part with some cash before you can download them (Fig 2). The payment process is simple through the Google Play store and, thanks to Google's own Wallet system, users can keep their details safe while purchasing as many apps as they like. Google does require you to input your card details to purchase apps, but you can always remove them by going directly into the settings menu within Google Play after purchasing all the apps you want at that time.

All the paid apps require just a one-off payment to download and each varies in its price. With some more of the expensive apps, such as CoPilot Live, you'll find that after purchasing the main app

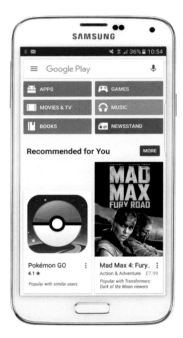

you will then have access to further content, like additional maps and routes, that can be purchased individually within the app. With so much on offer, you should download some apps right away!

Managing apps

After downloading some apps, the chances are that they will require an update at some point. Most apps automatically update themselves, if the setting is enabled, but the rest can be manually updated by going in to the My Apps section of the Play store (hit the Menu key for a quick shortcut). On the other hand, you might want to permanently delete an app from your device. In this case, simply go to its corresponding page on the Google Play store and select the Uninstall option. It's as easy as that.

Apps and games

The selection of apps on offer covers 27 different categories, so there's always something for everyone. Within each category of the Play store you can find the most downloaded apps within that section, as well as the highest rated ones. One particular area in which Android apps have vastly improved over the past year or so is in the quality of games that they now offer.

Many big brands have made the transition over to the smaller Android screen, with the likes of The Simpsons, Sonic The Hedgehog and Mass Effect to name but a few. There are also plenty of indie games that are Android exclusives and provide something quirky, original and compelling that you may not have experienced before. With so many games on offer, the downside is that they can take up lots of internal storage space on your device, so be careful not to download too many of them or you'll soon realise that you have precious little space for anything else.

Android games have their own dedicated section on the Play store for you to explore

Refund an app

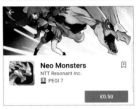

1 Find an app Go to the main information page of the app you want to download.

2 Purchase and download Tap the price, enter your payment details and download the app.

3 Trial period You now have 15 minutes to decide whether or not you want to keep the app.

4 Refund If you don't, go back to the app's page and then press the 'Refund' button.

| Google Play

Play Music

One of the biggest areas of the Google Play store that has expanded recently is the Play Music section (Fig 3). After signing contracts with numerous producers, Play Music now rivals the likes of iTunes and Spotify, especially with its new All Access subscription service. Singles and albums are competitively priced and you'll find all the latest chart hits ready for you to download. Each listing also has its own preview section that you can check out too. The companion to Play Music is the Google Play Music Manager desktop software, which enables users to upload all their tracks to Google's server and stream them from there. This stops you needing to take up valuable internal storage on your phone with your whole music library. The streaming service works really well and it's easy to create

Fig 3 (above) Album artwork looks fantastic within Play Music

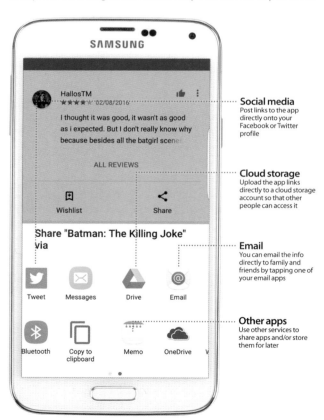

Social media
Post links to the app directly onto your Facebook or Twitter profile

Cloud storage
Upload the app links directly to a cloud storage account so that other people can access it

Email
You can email the info directly to family and friends by tapping one of your email apps

Other apps
Use other services to share apps and/or store them for later

Fig 4 (above) Play Books provides quick access to both the ebook you're reading and some recommended titles

Some of the biggest novels are free to download so keep an eye out for them

Share an app

playlists and perfect the sound quality using the built-in equaliser. If you've any sort of interest in music then Play Music is definitely something you need to check out.

1 Find an app Go to a specific app's information page on the Google Play store.

Play Books

Despite facing heavy competition from the likes of Amazon, Play Books has proved to be a big success on the Google Play store. With the Play Books app, you have instant access to the latest and greatest literature, all of which have been digitally optimised for your device (Fig 4). The selection is amazing and, no matter what your interests may be, there's something for everyone to download.

Prices are competitive and the download process takes all but a few minutes to complete, without taking up too much internal storage either. Each book can be read in Play Books' default reading app, which also works really well. Text can be customised to help your reading experience and you can even add virtual bookmarks so that you remember where you've read up to. If you're sick of lugging around heavy books with you, then Play Books is a brilliant solution for your literary needs that means you can carry a sprawling virtual library around with you everywhere you go.

2 Tap to share Scroll down and locate the share icon further down the page and then it.

3 Choose a route Scroll the pop-up list to find the share option you want to use and tap on it.

Enlarge text

1 Find settings While reading, tap the screen to bring up various display options around the page.

2 Which size? Choose the size option and then customise the text until it is more comfortable for you to read.

4 In the app Finish off the share process inside your chosen app and then it's job done.

The apps

Google Play

Rate an app

1 Download an app Download and install an app on your Galaxy phone or tablet.

2 Rate and review Tap on the 'Rate this app' button to start reviewing the app.

3 Add stars Give the app some feedback and a star rating, with five being the best score.

4 Post Add a message and then press OK to add your review to the list of other reviews.

Some films are also available for you to watch in HD so make sure you explore all the options

Play Newsstand

Google Play Newsstand is a new app that replaces Play Magazines and Google Currents by blending them together. It makes it easier to find and subscribe to magazines and mixes in suggested content from around the web based on what you've been reading. The more you read with the app, the smarter it gets and the more suggestions it can make. The first section is called Read Now and this contains suggested stories and subscribed news feeds. Tap on Read Now to see the other section headers which include My News, My Magazines, Bookmarks and Explore (Fig 5). Tap on Explore to see links to the Play Store, Featured news items, or sections of content such as entertainment, arts and photography, news and politics. Tap on one of these to see a choice of magazines or website to check out and subscribe to.

Play Movies

The final area of the Google Play store to explore is the Play Movies hub. As the name suggests, Play Movies contains the latest and greatest blockbuster titles that you can stream directly on your device, and in a few countries including the UK and US you can buy

Rent a film

1 Find a film Tap the search bar and enter the necessary keywords to find the film you want to rent.

2 Pay and watch Choose the 'Rent' option, pay for the movie and then sit back and enjoy.

48

TV shows as well. The service is pretty similar to the likes of Netflix but prices can be slightly cheaper depending on the movies that take your fancy. Once you've rented a movie you will have access to it for 24 hours, after which you will need to pay again to be able to watch. TV shows can be purchased per episode or per season.

Every purchase is tied directly to your Google account, meaning that you'll have access to it on any device that is also linked with the same account. Quality is great and if you're lucky enough to have a Samsung device with a Super AMOLED screen then your movie-viewing experience will be even better. If you're interested in getting the latest movies on your phone or tablet, look no further than the Play Movies hub where you'll find the history of Tinseltown right at your fingertips.

Fig 5 (above) Use Play Newsstand to download issues of your favourite magazines wherever you are

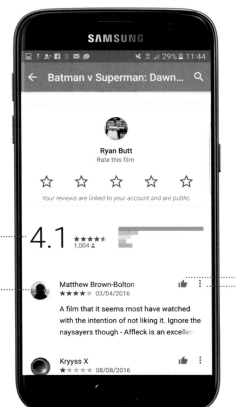

Average rating
At the top left of the ratings page is a quick summary showing you the average rating and the total number of ratings

Agree or disagree
Next to each review is a thumbs-up-and-down icon enabling you to choose if you agree or disagree with the review

Filter reviews
You can rearrange the reviews by how old they are and how helpful they are to you

Edit your review
Click on your own review to amend it and make edits to it where necessary

Galaxy Apps

Galaxy Apps

Fill your Samsung Galaxy device with the best apps around using Galaxy Apps

You'll use it to...

Download apps
Fill your Galaxy with different apps

Find recommendations
Get apps based on your search history

Get exclusive apps
Find apps only available for Galaxy users

Manage installations
Look through previously installed apps

Discover updates
Get the latest features for your most favourite apps

Explore Galaxy Apps

At its core, Galaxy Apps is a one-stop store for you to load your Galaxy device with the latest and greatest apps. Galaxy Apps now boasts an impressive number of titles to download, most of which are completely exclusive to the range of Samsung Galaxy devices, no matter if you happen to own a smartphone or tablet.

Discover and download apps

Look around Galaxy Apps and you'll find a wide array of both paid for and free apps (Fig 1). To make navigation easier,

Fig 1 (right) Galaxy Apps has plenty of titles to download

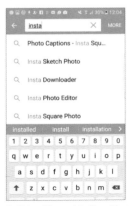

Fig 2 (above) The search tool is a quick way to find the app you want

each of these are organised into different categories. The process of downloading apps onto your Samsung Galaxy device is fairly simple, but does require several steps. First and foremost you'll need to find an app you want to download. You can do this by either using the search tool at the top of the app (Fig 2), or going through the correct category.

Once you've found the app you want, it's just a case of pressing the Download button and waiting for it to finish. If the app requires you to pay for it, and you've not paid for an app before, you'll be taken to a payment screen where you can enter card details. To take it one step further, you might also want to check out the reviews before downloading an app. Scroll to the bottom of an app's page and you can find genuine reviews posted by other Samsung Galaxy users who have downloaded it. Also on the app's page are other essential details, including who the developer is, how many downloads the app has had and the current version of the app. All of these points together will help you decide if this app is worth downloading on to your device.

Find exclusive Galaxy apps

While on the home page of Galaxy Apps, locate and press on the For Galaxy tab near the top of the page. You'll now be taken to the apps solely made for Samsung Galaxy devices. There's plenty on offer and you can find various types of apps as you scroll through. Many of the apps utilise specific features of various Galaxy devices. For example, this is the section you need to go to if you want to find compatible apps that work with your Galaxy Note's stylus, or apps that cater for the Samsung Galaxy S6's eye-tracking software.

Get the best Galaxy games

Galaxy Apps also provides a plethora of games. These range from big blockbuster titles, which have been ported over from other consoles, down to small independent games. The choice is superb and no matter what your tastes are, there's really something for everyone. One thing to keep an eye on is that although some games will be listed as free, once downloaded and installed you might need in-app purchases to unlock features within them.

Only update your apps over a Wi-Fi network because updating over 4G can use a lot of data

Download an app

1 Load app Search for an app or game and open up its own page on Galaxy Apps.

2 Permissions Press the Install button and read through the app permissions.

3 Downloading The app will download. Follow its progress on the Galaxy Apps page.

4 Review it After testing the app, leave a review by going to the bottom of the app's page.

Galaxy Apps

Master the Galaxy Apps settings

Although the main use of Galaxy Apps is to download apps, it's important to also take care of the store's settings. It may seem like a tedious task but without proper care, you could experience a massive slowdown on your device, apps not responding correctly and your battery life greatly reduced. Press on the menu icon at the top-left of the Galaxy Apps home page and select the Settings option from the bottom of the menu. The first setting you should change is the Password Protection option. This is a great way of stopping people from making unwarranted purchases on your account as it requires the password linked with your Samsung account to download the app. The next step is to make sure you're signed into your primary Samsung account at the bottom of the

Fig 3 (above) Manage your sync options from within the Settings app easily

Fig 4 (above) You'll find that downloading over 3G/4G will quickly use up your data allowance

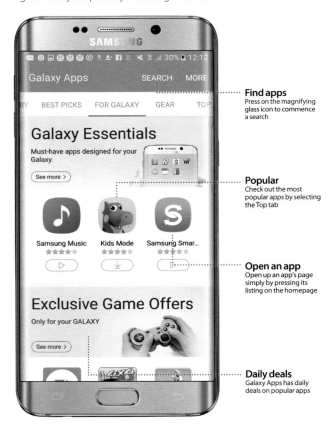

Find apps
Press on the magnifying glass icon to commence a search

Popular
Check out the most popular apps by selecting the Top tab

Open an app
Open up an app's page simply by pressing its listing on the homepage

Daily deals
Galaxy Apps has daily deals on popular apps

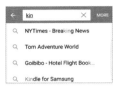

The search function is essential for finding a specific app that you know the name of

Settings menu. Downloading apps while signed into the wrong account will stop all downloaded apps from appearing when you eventually switch to the correct account.

The third and final essential change is disabling the Push Notifications option. This will prevent you receiving promotional messages regularly and can help save your battery life.

Keep all your apps updated

Now that you've filled your device with lots of apps and made some essential changes to how Galaxy Apps performs, you need to tackle how your device will update apps. By default, any app downloaded from Galaxy Apps will update automatically. Although this sounds good, it can actually lead to problems. Automatic app updates can drain your battery and it leaves you no choice but to accept the changes the update brings as well. Venture back into the Settings menu in Galaxy Apps and disable the choice to download apps automatically, which will put you back in control of how and when you update apps. To then manually update an app, simply go to that app's page and press on the Update button where the Install button is usually found.

Create an app wishlist

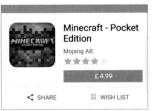

1 Add to Wish List Find an app that you want to add and then tap on the bookmark icon.

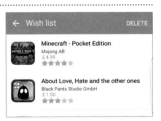

2 Access list On the main menu, tap 'More', followed by 'My Apps' and then tap on the Wish List option.

Share favourite apps

1 Open app page Open the page of one of your favourite apps on Galaxy Apps.

2 Open Share menu Press on the arrows icon at the top of the page to open the Share menu.

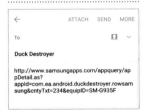

3 Share via email Press on one of the apps listed to share the link to a friend or contact.

4 S Memo Use S Memo to share and sync the app link with other Samsung devices.

Phone

You can do more than just call

You'll use it to...

Talk to people
Make phone calls

Quickly dial numbers
Set up a favourites list

Stop calls
Reject calls with an explanatory SMS

Restrict calls
Set up blacklists to stop cold-callers

Find connections
Search for your contacts easily

Connect quicker
Set up speed dials

Using your phone

Whatever else your Galaxy can do, it will be able to make and take phone calls. That's the essence of any phone, and your Galaxy manages to do it very well indeed. Part of this is its ability to handle huge numbers of contacts; it manages reams of information about them, including details of all the calls you've made.

Keypad and Contacts

While the keypad of your Galaxy might look, at first, as though you have to do all the work entering in the numbers each time you make a call (Fig 1), that's not the case. You don't

Fig 1 (right) No matter how little data you have left to spend of your allowance, you'll always be able to place a phone call

Fig 2 (above) It is easy to find specific contacts by using the dial pad

have to remember the phone number of every person you know – your Galaxy does that for you. You can designate some contacts as 'favourite' people and they'll be listed under the Favourites tab inside the Phone app, while the full list of everyone whose details you've saved is listed under the Contacts tab.

However, you don't have to rifle through your contacts every time you want to call somebody. Just go straight to the Keypad screen. Work with the letters on each key rather than the numbers, and start tapping out any part of someone's name. Matches are shown on-screen – the matching letters will be highlighted in blue

(Fig 2). If there is more than one match then you can tap the drop-down arrow to the right to see them all or keep typing until there is just one match. When you've found who you need, tap the green dial button to make a call or the video call button instead.

Logs and Favourites
Your Galaxy remembers who you have called and it is easy to see this information. If you ever need to refer to your call history, just hit the Logs tab along the top of the Phone app. On the Logs screen you can see how many times you've made and received calls to and from a number, and tapping a number gives you even more details, as well as a shortcut to their Contacts page and some dial buttons.

Meanwhile, you can set up your favourite people in the Contacts app and get to these by tapping the Favourites button. You could use this for your closest friends and family so that reaching them is only ever a couple of screen taps away.

Call settings
When you are in the Phone app, tap on the Menu button beneath the device's screen area to bring up options including Call settings. Tap that and you'll be able to set up a wide range of different options that help you personalise how you make and take calls.

There are some really useful options here. Turning the screen off during calls is great if you spend time in places where the screen might irritate other people, like cinemas. You can set different ways to answer and end calls too – perhaps you prefer using the Power button to end a call, for example. There's a useful setting that gets your Galaxy to raise its ringtone volume when it is in your pocket or bag, so you stand a better chance of hearing it in crowded places.

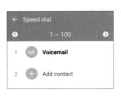

Tap the Menu button while on the Keypad screen then Speed dial to access these

Make a call

1 Go to the keypad Tap the Phone icon on your home screen to open the dialer.

2 Identify the caller Tap out the name of the person you want to ring, then tap the Call button.

3 Use the speaker While you are inside the call, tap Speaker to enable the speakerphone.

4 Volume If the caller sounds faint, turn up the volume and use the extra volume button.

Phone

Create a blacklist

There may be certain people who have your mobile number but who you'd rather not take calls from. Whether they are ex-partners, old clients or pesky call centres, we all have certain numbers we'd like to block from our phones. Instead of having to manually stop a call each time you're called, you can set up a blacklist of numbers whose calls will automatically be rejected (Fig 3).

In the Phone app, tap the Menu button that is located at the top of the screen and then select the Settings. Next, tap Cell>Call rejection and make sure that the slider for Auto reject mode is showing green. If it is grey then the function won't work, so simply slide it to the right to ensure that you're able to block numbers. Next, tap Auto reject list.

Contacts
Tap here to jump across to the Contacts app

Favourites
Tap on this tab to see all of your favourite contacts

Logs
Check here for information about past incoming and outgoing calls

Video or voice?
Tap one of these to make a video or a voice call

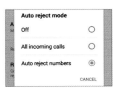

If you want to use Auto reject mode, you must ensure it is turned on in the settings

If you check 'Unknown' then all calls from anyone who is not listed in your contacts will automatically be rejected. Be careful if you do this as some companies and establishments' numbers are never displayed. If you would like to add a specific number to the blacklist then tap Create and add a number. Tap the photo icon to search call logs or contacts for a specific number, or just type a number into the box. Finally, tap Save to activate your blacklist.

1 Set up speed dials From the Keypad screen, press the Menu button then Speed dial.

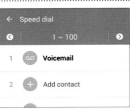

Set auto-reject text

Sometimes a call comes in and you are interested in talking to that particular person, but you just can't take the call immediately for whatever reason. However, it is possible to let them know you are interested in talking rather than just sending their call directly to voicemail. Your Galaxy lets you set up text messages that you can easily send out as you are rejecting a call.

Once again, press the Menu button to bring up the options and then choose Call Settings. Tap Set reject messages. There are several template messages already in the system but you can easily add personalised ones by tapping Create. When a call comes in you can then reject it by sending a pre-written text message.

2 Select a number Tap one of the speed dial numbers that's not yet been allocated.

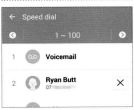

3 Add a contact Search for a contact in your list to add to the speed dial.

Automatically reject calls

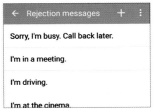

1 Set up SMS Go to Settings> Call> Call rejection and tap on Rejection messages to create or select one.

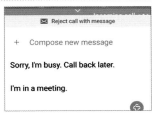

2 Reject the call When you reject a call, select a specific message to let the caller know you can't answer.

4 Use speed dial Once added, call them by long-pressing their number on the keypad.

Contacts

Manage the details of your friends, family and colleagues in the Contacts app

You'll use it to…

Manage contacts
Keep track of everyone important

Organise groups
Put similar contacts together

Merge sources
Link information from multiple apps

Set ringtones
Give your friends a personal ringer

Mark favourites
Highlight contacts for quick access

Manage calls
Place calls or send texts directly

Fig 1 (right) You can keep all of your favourite contacts on a screen widget

Fig 2 (above) You can manually add people to your Contacts app

Keeping up with contacts

One of the most handy functions on any phone is the ability to keep all your contact details in one place, in the process enabling you to keep in touch with your friends (Fig 1). Your Galaxy device can be used to bring together information about your contacts from a whole range of sources.

Create new contacts

There are lots of ways to add contacts to your Galaxy device; you can import them from places like your Google, Facebook or Samsung ChatON

accounts; import contacts from a SIM, or simply add them manually. In order to do this, all you have to do is go into the Contacts app and tap the plus sign next to the search box near the top of the screen. After this, all that's left to do is add information (Fig 2).

You are given a simple set of fields at first, like name, mobile number, email address and home address. However, should you wish to, you can expand these to add multiple numbers, email addresses and home addresses. You can assign a contact to a group such as work, family or friends, and in the process attach a dedicated ringtone and vibration pattern to them.

Contacts

Once these basic tasks have been completed, you can add more fields such as website, organisation and even attach notes, as well as change the contact's photo by tapping on it. Manually adding contacts in this way is slower and arguably less efficient than simply adding them in bulk from existing accounts, but it is very useful if you need to add or edit specific details, or you meet new people.

Add an app account

A great way to import contacts to your Galaxy device is to do so through an app. One example is to add your Facebook account so that the contacts you have there are drawn into the device's contacts. In order to do this, go to your main Settings app, then scroll down to Accounts and select the Add Account option. Select Facebook from the list, install the app and then log in. Having done this, you will be asked to set the sync preferences, after which synchronisation will commence automatically and your data will move across.

Import/export contacts

Contacts can be imported to and exported from a range of different places. You might find that exporting contacts to USB storage represents a good way to make a local physical backup from time to time, or you may feel more secure leaving such data in the cloud. Moreover, it also means that if you are upgrading from an older phone and want to import the contacts you've got on your SIM, then you can do so easily and without fuss.

In order to import or export your contacts, first open Contacts and make sure that you are in the main Contacts view screen. After you've done this, tap the Menu button. On the screen that pops up, select Import/Export and make your choice.

If you're importing contacts from a SIM, send them to Google so they'll sync with your Galaxy

The apps

Join or split contacts

1 Two people, one contact Importing contacts can often result in duplicated information.

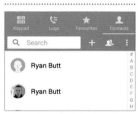

2 Start the link Hit the linked chain icon by the Connections section to see linked accounts.

3 Find the connection Tap Link another contact and you will receive a recommendation.

4 Join more Join more together if you need to and view the entries from the contact page.

The apps

Contacts

Fig 3 (above) It's easy to split your list of contacts down into manageable groups

Fig 4 (above) You can send text messages and emails out en masse, if you like

Set up groups

Once you have all your contacts in place, you might want to set up some groups (Fig 3). This represents a great way of keeping people you deal with in a particular way together. Perhaps you have a special group of friends or a family group, or maybe a set of work colleagues that you like to group together. Doing this is easy with your Galaxy device, which comes with a number of groups set up already, and also gives you the facility through which to create even more groups quickly and easily. Simply hit the Menu key from the Groups page, select Create, give your group a name and a specific ringtone or vibration pattern if desired, and finally tap Add member at the bottom of the page. From there you can simply select the people you wish to add and then hit Done at the top-right.

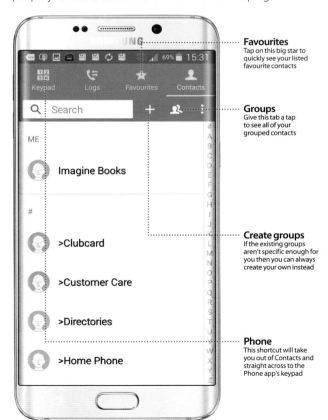

Favourites
Tap on this big star to quickly see your listed favourite contacts

Groups
Give this tab a tap to see all of your grouped contacts

Create groups
If the existing groups aren't specific enough for you then you can always create your own instead

Phone
This shortcut will take you out of Contacts and straight across to the Phone app's keypad

60

When choosing contacts to display, tap the settings icon beside Customised List to specify groups

You can very easily add to and delete from these groups as time goes on so that they can reflect your ever-evolving circles of friends and your social life. Sometimes, though, a group won't cover it if you need to contact a bunch of people who aren't usually connected. In this case, hit the Menu key from the main contacts list and select Send email or Send message. You can then select recipients (Fig 4).

Customise the list

As you can probably appreciate, you can easily end up with a lot of contacts stored on your Galaxy device, and it is highly likely that you won't actually need to see them all at any given time. To help you get to grips with a very large contacts list, you can customise it so that not all of the contacts are available to view at once. You might not want to make a customisation setting and use it all the time, but it could be something that you use to filter through your large list and make it more manageable.

For example, you can choose to narrow down your contacts so that only those sourced from a particular place, such as your SIM or Facebook account, are displayed. Alternatively, you can produce a list that has been more heavily customised.

Customise contacts display

1 Menu option Tap the menu icon and go to Settings then select Contacts and tap Contacts to display.

2 Make selection Decide which contacts you want to display – you can even customise the settings.

Set Favourite contacts

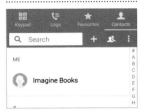

1 Mark contacts as favourite To begin with, open up the Contacts app.

2 Select a contact Now pick a contact who is important to you so you can add them to the list.

3 Star the contact Tap the star at the top-right of the contact page so that it becomes yellow.

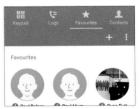

4 View favourites Tap Favourites at the top of the Contacts screen to see your starred contacts.

Messaging

Get to grips with messaging on your Galaxy

You'll use it to...

Text people
Send and receive text messages

Share images
Attach pictures to MMS messages

Dictate messages
Save time and keep your hands free

Stay organised
Manage spam messages

Reply with templates
Send short pre-written messages

Customise alerts
Set your own message notifications

Fig 1 (right) Messaging provides you with threaded conversations so that you don't have to keep digging through old texts

Fig 2 (above) Tap on a phone number inside a text message to either call the sender or add them as a contact

Texting friends and family

Texting is one of the most popular uses of any phone and your Galaxy has texting down to a fine art. It's easy to take advantage of its simple and accessible interface to keep in touch with all your family and friends (Fig 1).

Send a text message

Texting is about a lot more than just creating and sending messages. Suppose someone sends you a website address in a text message – it becomes a live link and you can tap it to go straight to the

site. Alternatively, if someone texts you a phone number then just tapping it will bring up a menu from which you can call them or add them to your contacts (Fig 2).

There's another potentially useful item on that menu too: copy message text. Imagine you want to take a bit of an SMS and put it into an email, or even send text from one SMS to a new recipient – with this command you can copy the text and then paste it straight into any other app that supports text.

SMS messages are 'threaded', meaning that you can see a conversational view between you and the person you are chatting to. You might not always want to keep every message, though, and if you long-press on any particular message you can delete it. You also get the option to forward the message on to someone else or lock it so it can't be accidentally removed, which is great for tickets.

Attach photos and videos

Messaging is often just about text, but it doesn't have to be. It is easy to attach a picture or video to a text message, and in doing so convey so much more. If you take a photo that you want to share, start a text message and then hit the attachment icon beside the typing area – it looks like a paperclip. Now go to Images, then Gallery and select the photo you want to attach. It'll be embedded within the body of the message, which is upgraded from SMS to MMS, and you can send it when ready.

Message and display settings

You can make use of a range of settings to help you get more out of the SMS messages you send and receive. In the main Messaging window, tap the Menu button on your device to see a number of options, including Settings. Tap this and you can make all kinds of changes to how your messages look and are managed.

You can switch between different viewing styles for messages and change the font size too, helping you squeeze more onto the screen at once. You can also tell the handset to automatically delete older messages if you get past the limit for messages in any one text conversation. This helps you manage the storage memory of your device automatically.

So as we have seen, texting on your Galaxy is a simple exercise that will soon become as effortless as breathing. Just take a few moments to explore the range of options available and, once your first text has been sent, you'll be completely familiar with the setup and the procedure.

Tap menu and choose Quick responses to send standardised responses to any messages you receive

Dictate an SMS

1 Start SMS Open Messaging and tap the Compose button at the top-right of the screen.

2 Enter recipient Enter the recipient(s) details in the box at the top of the screen.

3 Voice entry Long-press the cog icon to the left of the space bar then tap the microphone icon.

4 Speak your text Now speak and your words will be instantly turned into an SMS message.

Messaging

Notifications, signatures and spam

There are other settings you can make to help you get more from your messages. On the main Messaging screen tap the Menu button beneath the screen and then select Settings. Then scroll down the screen to see the full range of settings available (Fig 3). You can request a delivery report so you can be absolutely certain your message has arrived at the other end, and you can even get a notification when the message has been opened by the recipient.

You can also make a range of settings to notify when you have received an SMS, including repeating incoming message alerts, setting a ringtone notification and getting a preview of a message on the notifications bar at the top of your device's screen. That's useful if you don't want to go into the Messaging app to get the

Fig 3 (above) You can make sophisticated settings for managing text messages and tailoring the app to suit your needs

Recipients
All your recipients are listed in this area at the top of the screen

Composing a message
You've got 160 characters for each message, and you can see a countdown here

Predictive text
It can be faster to tap the word you want when it appears here rather than type the whole thing

Tools
Access tools like handwriting and speech recognition here

Selecting a ringtone for your incoming messages can help you distinguish your phone from others

gist of what they are about. You can also block senders and register particular phrases that block messages – this is handy if you get a lot of SMS spam on a particular topic. You can even add a short signature to your SMS messages.

Add emoji

We often use shorthand when writing SMS messages to save on characters, since we're only allowed 160, as well as to make typing faster. We've also become addicted to emoji, the little characters that express how we're feeling. Happy and sad faces are the most frequently used, but there are lots more. Your Galaxy has a host of them built in, covering a wide range of different sentiments: laughter, confusion, indecision, foot-in-mouth, surprise and more.

You can enter these into a text message using the characters that combine to make them. For example, :-) makes up a happy face and :-[is the combination for the embarrassed emoji. If you type these into a message then its Android symbol is sent instead of the constituent characters. However, it's more fun and often faster to use the menu to send emoji instead. Plus, you won't have to remember lots of different combinations of keys.

Find the emoji

1 Emoji menu When writing a message tap the emoji face icon to the left of the text field.

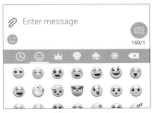

2 Insert emoji Pick an emoji to insert by tapping on it and it will instantly appear in your message.

Handwrite a message

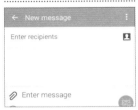

1 Handwrite a message Tap to open Messaging and then opt to start a new message.

2 Select handwriting Long-press the button to the left of the space bar and choose the 'T'.

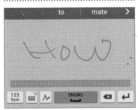

3 Start to write Write your message in the text area that appears using your fingertip.

4 Symbols Use the symbol key to place additional symbols inside your message text.

Hangouts

Use Google's own Hangouts service to keep in contact with friends and family

You'll use it to…

Chat to friends
Send unlimited free messages to your friends and contacts

Work on projects with your contacts
Edit and share documents in real time

Manage multiple accounts
Sync all your contacts into a single account

Start video calls
Create free video calls with contacts

Talk to several contacts at the same time
Add people to your conversations

Add funny effects to videos
Implement funny edits to your video chat

Fig 1 (right) Your contacts are arranged by most frequently contacted people up top

Fig 2 (above) Use the front-facing camera on your phone to start a video call

Chatting with Google Hangouts

At its core, Google Hangouts is a cross-platform messaging service that allows you to have text and video chats with your friends and contacts from your Galaxy device (Fig 1). You can send emoji and animated GIFs, send and receive text messages within the app, and switch between SMS and Hangouts. The app is now available on iOS too.

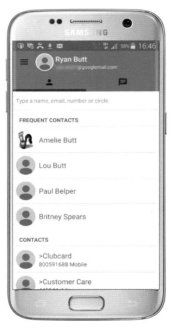

Make a video call

With so many apps now available from both the Samsung App and Google Play stores, there's a real plethora of video call apps available for download. The likes of WhatsApp and Skype now have millions of users using their video call functions on a daily basis completely free of charge and, although Hangouts doesn't yet have that amount of avid followers, it does include a selection of cool features that can be applied to its very own video call function.

Setting up a video call within Hangouts is easy enough; all that's required is for both you and your specified contact to have a front facing camera on each device (Fig 2). You also need to make sure the contact has Google's Hangouts app installed on their device, or that they are signed in to the web service. After that, just tap on a contact to select them and pick the video option. Once connected you can then control your audio, switch between your front and back cameras, and enjoy a video chat with up to ten of your friends.

Use in-chat options

Hangouts includes a few in-chat options, located in the top and bottom bars, that you can use to improve the quality of your chat. The main in-chat options deal with the audio, allowing you to choose between speakers and headphones or Bluetooth devices, and you can also disable the video link and return to a text chat if your connection is a little poor. If you decide to pop over to your desktop computer and sign in to the web service then you can even add fun effects to your videos.

Change the settings

As with any app of this type, you'll want to have a range of settings that you can tinker with to perfect how the app functions, and while the Hangouts app isn't yet as fully featured as its predecessor, Talk, you can still access the main settings.

You'll find options enabling you to control the notifications that you receive from the app, how people can make contact with you and also the blocking of people you don't want to hear from. If you want to change any of the settings related to your Google+ account, or quickly nip across to set up a new circle, then tap the Google+ profile heading under Account and navigate from there. Hangouts works from inside of Gmail as well so take a break from writing an email and make a video call with a friend.

Hangouts is a versatile and incredibly useful app that will allow you to communicate quickly and easily with your loved ones. Long face-to-face video calls or quick text chats – the choice is yours.

The Snooze notifications option in the settings lets you silence noisy conversations for a while

New request settings

1 Hangouts Hit the Menu button while on the app's main home screen and select Settings.

2 Settings On the next screen, scroll down to Customise invites, just above Account.

3 Requests Tap the option to see the various types of people who can get in touch with you.

4 Set the limits Tap each group to choose whether or not they can start a Hangout with you.

Email

The Samsung Galaxy offers many options for email, one of the most important communication features

You'll use it to…

Send messages
Send and receive emails while on the go

Share photos
You can attach images to your emails…

Share videos
… and even video files, too!

Contact multiple people
You can send a single message to more than one individual simultaneously

Manage accounts
Use different email accounts for different purposes

Dictate emails
You can use the mic to record your message

Fig 1 (right) Setting up your Email app is a very simple process

Fig 2 (above) On the main email screen, tap on the Inbox button at the top to switch between inboxes from different accounts

Managing multiple email accounts

There are obvious benefits to using multiple email accounts during your day-to-day life, and the ability to do this is right at the heart of Samsung's Email app. It is a very useful option to have because it allows you to organise your emails into different categories, the most obvious being one email account for work-related emails and then another for your personal life.

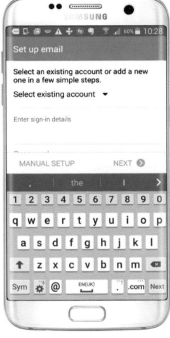

Add an account

Adding an email account to your Galaxy device is very easy. In order to do so, just go to your Email app and press the Inbox button in the top-left corner of the screen. A pop-up menu will appear listing various options, including your combined inboxes, priority senders and sent emails. Tap on Manage accounts at the bottom of the screen and here you can manage your accounts individually by tapping on them or add a new account by tapping the '+' icon in the top-right corner of the screen. This is where you will be able to input details of your new email account (Fig 1). There are two input boxes available. Type your required email address at the top and your password into the bottom box. If need be, you can tap the Show Password

Email | The apps

box if you are unsure about your typing skills and would like to seek reassurance. If you want this email account to be your default one then tap on the next box down: Send email from this account by default. Tap Next and your phone will subsequently negotiate a series of checks. Select your Account Option, tap Next and then Done. You can switch accounts by tapping the Inbox button (Fig 2).

Customise email display

With this option, you can easily customise your email application so that it better suits your life, if you so desire. Tap on the Menu key, which will cause a pop-up menu to appear. After doing this, tap on Filter By – this will allow you to sort your emails by various categories, such as Unread or Read, by whether they are highlighted by a star, their priority or by those with attachments linked to them – plenty of filter options to choose from! From the menu icon you can also organise your email into the regular listings or link them into a conversational mode. As well as this, you have the ability to increase or decrease the font size and manage your email's storage folders.

Respond to emails

When new emails arrive in your inbox, tap on them in order to read them. Once you have done that, you can choose to respond by tapping on the single left-curving arrow. Just type in your response and tap the envelope icon up at the top-right to send. You can also forward information to a contact by tapping the straight right arrow. Moreover, you can also choose to move your message to a desired folder. Just highlight your message within the Inbox, tap the menu icon next to the sender at the top of the screen and choose the folder into which you would like to move the email.

To sort messages, tap the menu icon and choose Select. Then pick emails and sort with the icons

View saved emails

1 Save email Within your displayed email, tap the Menu button and then Save email.

2 App menu To view saved emails, exit the Email app and return to the App Drawer.

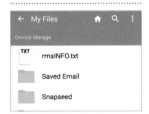

3 My Files Tap the My Files app, then 'Device storage'. Look for the Saved Email folder.

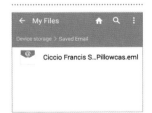

4 View mail You'll see a list of folders. Scroll to Save Email and tap on it to view your email files.

Email

Fig 3 (above) Use the array of formatting options to modify your email text

Compose an email

Composing new emails is quick and easy through the Email app. While in an inbox, you will see a pencil and paper icon in the lower-left corner. Tap on this icon to be taken to the email composition screen. You need to insert the recipient's email address in the To box and then next to the word Subject, tap and type in the topic of your email. Now, you can think about what you are going to say within your email. Tap the large white area of the screen and begin typing your email using the on-screen keyboard. Use the formatting options by tapping the arrow icon to modify your text (Fig 3). You might, for example, want to highlight a word or portion of text and then tap on the B button within the formatting band – this will embolden your text. Similarly, you can tap on the Undo and Redo

Attach
The paperclip icon is the attachment button that lets you send various media along with your message

Send
The envelope icon with the arrow running through it is the Send command, which dispatches your emails

Formatting bar
The formatting bar allows you to modify the look of your email text and insert objects into it

Message area
The white area in the centre of the screen is where your text resides

Fig 4 (above) If you tap the menu icon while writing a new email then you'll have access to even more options, like Priority

Attach a map

You can decide not to send a message. Tap the back button on your device and 'Discard'

1 Write email Open up the Email app and write your email, attaching the relevant addresses.

buttons in case of errors and also insert a number of elements, such as images, memos and contacts, via the Insert button beside them. Tap the envelope icon at the top of the screen to send your email.

Additional sending options

You can send an email in a straightforward manner or modify your sending options. Within the composition screen, tap on the menu icon and a range of new options will appear on the pop-up menu (Fig 4). You can send an email to yourself or to others to provide copies of the email to those who need them. Schedule email allows you to send an email at a specified date and time, while the Priority option allows you to mark each message with a low, normal or high priority status to grade the importance of each message. Finally, you also have the option of introducing Security options within your sent email, such as the option to Encrypt the email to secure its contents and ensure that only the intended recipient ever sees it. If you wish to abandon an email during composition, you can either tap the back button on your device or tap the 'X' icon on the top row of options. This latter method doesn't even ask if you are sure, which can save you time.

2 Insert Tap the Insert icon, situated third from the left on the formatting bar.

3 Location Tap on the Maps icon that is found within the pop-up menu box.

Attaching items

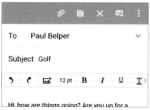

1 Tap paperclip While composing an email, tap on the paperclip icon in the top-left corner.

2 Select attachment You will be presented with a screen full of services to attach an item from.

4 Map Decide to include your current location or find a map reference to feature.

Internet

Explore the vast resources of the internet with your Samsung Galaxy device

You'll use it to…

Browse the web
Explore a world of information

Save information
Retain information for offline viewing

Download files
Enjoy music, videos, images and more

View multiple websites
Keep multiple website windows open at the same time while browsing

Stay private
Manage your privacy settings to keep you safe online

Create shortcuts
Add Home Screen links for quick access

Fig 1 (right) You can input both search terms, to be processed by a search engine, and URLs into the multibar at the top

Fig 2 (above) The keyboard is a multifunction affair that can save you time

Browsing the web

The Internet app is one of the native apps that arrives pre-loaded onto your Samsung Galaxy. It is your window onto the internet, allowing you to roam the worldwide web wherever you are and, in the process, access a wealth of information that you can view and manipulate. You can even set up shortcuts to any websites that you frequently visit so that they sit on your home screen like any other app shortcut, which is perfect for enabling speedy access to your favourite web watering holes. With the Internet app, there are no boundaries.

Navigate with the multibar

The heart of the Internet app is the multibar. This is the area of the app in which you can not only search the internet, but also input website addresses (Fig 1). If you decide to use the space as a search engine then, when you begin to type out your search words, the app will try to second-guess your instructions. This means that every time you add another letter to the words you are typing, the search engine will present a selection of results based on those letters. Tap on the result to go to the connected website.

Alternatively, you can simply enter a website address if you have a particular location in mind. The keyboard keys can be utilised to speed up the instructions (Fig 2). For example, there is a '.com' button available that reflects just how common this notation is during website address entries, while tapping the settings icon will take you directly to the keyboard settings area. Also, tap on the bottom left key to be taken to a numbers and symbols layout. Tap on the 1/2 key above in order to see further symbolic selections.

Home screen shortcuts

1 Options Within the Internet app, tap the More button while on the website of your choice.

Switch between tabs

If you are adept at multitasking then you may be pleased to hear that you can examine more than one website at a time. In order to open a new website window, tap on the Tabs icon to the right of the bar at the bottom of the screen. Tap 'New Tab' to open a new window. Tap on the Tabs icon again and swipe up or down to examine each window, switching between tabs in the process. Tap the Tabs icon and choose 'Enable Secret' option to utilise a window that creates no records in your browser or search history, thus adding extra privacy enhancements to hide your browsing history.

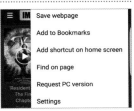

2 Bookmark page Tap the 'Add shortcut on home screen' option and it will be added.

3 Home screen To check, exit the Internet app and search through your home screens to find it.

Use your History and Bookmarks

If you wish to retain your place on the web so that you can revisit a website without having to search for it all over again, just tap on the Bookmarks icon that sits at the bottom of the screen and then tap on the 'Add' option. You can also access your saved pages at any point by tapping the Bookmarks icon at the bottom of the screen. While on the Bookmarks screen, you may notice the History tab at the top of the screen. Tap on this to see which websites you have been looking at previously, and browse through a timeline of your Internet activity.

4 Final shortcut Tap on the shortcut to go directly to the indicated website.

To clear your history, while in the History tab in Bookmarks, tap More then 'Clear history'

Internet

Fig 3 (above) The Advanced settings contain a number of useful options to help customise your web experience

Control zoom and font size

Your Galaxy has the ability to modify just about every aspect of your device and its interface. For example, you can change the zoom function and how you control it. Yes, there is the familiar spread and pinch to zoom in and out, but you can also add extra control. Tap the More icon in the top-right corner of the interface and scroll to Settings. Now tap the 'Manual zoom' category (Fig 3) and move the slider to the 'On' position, which overrides a website's request to control zoom behaviour.

You can also change the font size to aid ease of use here. To do this, tap on the Advanced option within the primary Settings screen followed by the Text Size option (Fig 4). Now move the Text scaling slider to change the way that text is resized. This should make

Fig 4 (above) Changing the font size will provide you with better accessibility when you are browsing the web

More options
Tap here to bring up options to add new bookmarks, save pages to your Home screen and more

Multibar
Use this area as both a search bar and to directly input a website address

Bookmarks
Tap on the Bookmark icon at the bottom-right of the screen to save a page for later

Tabs
You can have several tabs open in the app, and you can open a new one by tapping this icon

Change your home page by going to Settings and then tapping on the Homepage option

it easier for you to read the text on certain websites. You can, of course, adjust this option at any time to suit your needs.

Manage your downloads

Once you download information from the internet, how do you manage it? What happens if you download several pieces? Can you move the information elsewhere after you have downloaded it? All these things are possible with the associated app called My Files. When you download something from the internet, a small pulsating down-facing arrow appears in your notifications bar. Go to the My Files app to see the result. Tap to enter and then tap on the Download history category to see all of your downloaded files. Each will feature an icon indicating how you can play or view the download. Tap the download to start that associated app, or instead tap the menu icon and choose the Sort by option to arrange files by date, name or size. Press and hold on a downloaded file to highlight them and then either tap on the trashcan icon to delete them or the share icon at the top of the screen to move them to the likes of Dropbox, Email, Wi-Fi Direct and Bluetooth. The process is quick and very easy to get to grips with.

Delete downloads

1 Highlight files To delete your downloads, press and hold on a file and highlight it with a tick.

2 Delete After selecting the files you wish to delete, tap on the 'Remove' option to delete.

Save for offline reading

1 Select website Choose the page of the website that you would like to save.

2 Options Hit the More icon and tap the Save page option from the pop-up menu.

3 Save page Your saved page will then be confirmed with an on-screen notification.

4 Access page To access your saved pages, tap Bookmarks then the Saved Pages tab.

Camera

Save space on gadgets by using your Samsung Galaxy device as a camera

You'll use it to…

Take pictures
Capture moments while on the move

Shoot video
Record videos with your device

Get up close
Zoom right into your images

Share photos
Send your snaps via email and more

Print photos
Print out your images via Wi-Fi or USB

Become a pro
Use a variety of professional camera modes

Fig 1 (right) The Camera app will automatically focus on your subject

Fig 2 (above) Open up the camera and adjust the settings before you start taking photos

Using the camera

To use the camera, you will need to access your App Drawer and tap on the Camera icon. Now aim the main camera lens at your desired subject and make any necessary adjustments that you may require before pressing the shutter button at the bottom of the screen in order to take the actual picture. If you would like to record a video instead, just tap on the video camera icon next to the shutter button and video will automatically record.

Take your first picture

Taking your first picture will reveal just how powerful the camera feature is on your Samsung Galaxy. When you open the app, you will be presented with a host of features that can affect your final image. In low light, for example, the flash feature is an essential inclusion. The zigzag arrow in the quick settings can be used to change this mode. Tap on either Off, On or Auto flash if you want the camera itself to make the call as to whether or not the flash function should be utilised. Of course, you may choose to simply take a picture of what's in front of you, but you might also want to capture an image of yourself. With this in mind, the option exists for you to toggle the front and back camera in order to easily and accurately take a self-portrait. In order to do this, tap on the camera icon in the top-right corner of the screen to switch between the front and rear-facing cameras. Zooming into your subject is very easy: simply place two fingers on the screen and slowly spread them apart. To zoom out, pinch them together.

Share pictures immediately

Once you've taken a picture tap its thumbnail at the bottom-right corner of the screen to open the Gallery, followed by the Share icon at the top of the screen, then select a share option such as Bluetooth, Dropbox or Email. To share images with friends, tap the share icon, followed by Wi-Fi Direct. Here, select the user that you want to connect to and then the selected images will be forwarded to the connected device quickly and easily.

Apply effects and night mode

Being able to take photos on your device is all well and good. However, you should also be aware that you can add a little bit more of a spark to your work by enhancing it with the various additional modes and effects that are available. Tap on the Settings cog in the top-left corner of the screen and tap Effects in order to access a range of photo filter effects. Press and swipe sideways to scroll through the various filters. Tap on a filter to apply that effect. In fact, before you even take a picture, you can cycle through each of the different effects to see how it will turn out if you apply it to the image. You can manage your effects by scrolling all the way to the right and choosing the Manage Effects option to determine which effects you want displayed. You can also tap on Download to get more effects from Galaxy Apps.

More effects can be downloaded for free from the Galaxy Apps store that you can visit in-app

Shoot a video

1 Adjust Tap on Settings and make required adjustments to video stabilisation and more.

2 Switch Tap on the video recorder icon to switch modes and start recording footage.

3 Focus Tap where you want to focus. This will cause the focus box to change to a green colour.

4 Record The video will start recording straight away. Tap the Stop button to cease recording.

Camera

Explore shooting modes

The built-in camera can take photos in the same way as any other camera with a single shot. There are, however, other shooting modes that can add a welcome level of variation, and Best Photo does just that. The camera will take eight pictures, and subsequently ask you to choose the best to save from the listed thumbnails. Best Face takes five photos of a person, and then presents you with a selection of faces, from which you can choose the best one to save.

Moreover, there's a face detection mode that allows you to take a picture of a person and then, when the camera detects and places a square around the face, tap on it to zoom into the face and then take a sharp close-up picture. There is also the panorama option, which works almost like a combination of the camera and video

Fig 3 (above) The various shooting modes available in the Camera app offer more flexibility when taking photos

Menu bar
The menu bar at the top of the screen (S4/S5) features your most popular settings. This bar can be modified

Settings
The cogwheel icon on the top-left of the screen is your entry point to a host of settings

Picture thumbnail
The tiny image in the bottom-left is your most recent picture. Tap to view it inside the Gallery app

Shutter button
Take a photo by pressing this button. When in video mode, the camera image turns into a red button

Tap Download in the Effects settings to find a selection of other free effects to download

modes, in that you use the camera to take a long, sweeping image, in the process producing one very long photograph. To access the various modes, simply tap the Mode button in the lower-left corner and then scroll through the various options. What's more, if you scroll down to the bottom of the list you will find the option to download more modes.

1 Settings In the Camera app, tap the Menu button to reveal the Edit shortcuts option.

Change the camera settings
While in the app, enter the Settings mode. Since the menu sits in a floating box, it's not immediately obvious that you can scroll to the further settings below. Some of the settings available include Exposure value, which is a sort of manual Scene mode; a Macro or Auto focus mode; a timer that you can set between two and ten seconds for picture-taking; and also an ISO setting, which affects the shutter speed by taking into account the available light. Anti-Shake should prevent blurry images while the White balance gives you a choice between Daylight, Cloudy, Incandescent or Fluorescent.

Other useful settings include Metering, Outdoor visibility, Auto contrast, Guidelines (which places a grid on the screen according to the rule of thirds) and GPS tagging to locate your images.

2 Tap shortcut Press and hold on a shortcut to open the shortcut edit window.

GPS tag

3 Select icon Tap and drag an icon into a shortcut placeholder to add it to your shortcuts list.

Attention

Enabling Location tags will attach, embed, and store geographical location data within each picture that you take. Use caution when you send, share, distribute, transmit, or copy these pictures since they contain information about where the picture was taken.

1 Settings In the Camera app, tap on the Settings and scroll down to the Location tag option.

2 Locate your pic Tap this option to turn it on and your pictures will now be tagged.

4 Remove Shortcuts You can also remove items from the menu by dragging them out.

Gallery

The Gallery app isn't just a place for storing photos and videos, as you'll soon discover

You'll use it to…

Store media files
Take full advantage of the various different storage albums

Tag your friends
Use Tag Buddy to put names to faces

Edit your photos
Perform simple editing techniques on your photos

Upload to social media sites
Enable auto-uploading of your photos to Facebook

Share videos wirelessly
Use Kies to wirelessly share videos

Personalise your Galaxy
Apply a photo or video as wallpaper

Fig 1 (right) The carousel view is a unique way to display your photos in a dynamic and engaging way

Fig 2 (above) The Gallery app now links to some great photo editing tools that you can explore and play around with

Viewing photos

The Gallery app fundamentally does what its name suggests; it offers a great way of simply viewing all your photos. In recent updates the Gallery app has now expanded into areas of photo editing and video management (Fig 1).

Navigate your albums

Whenever you save a photo or video on your Galaxy device, it's automatically added to a default album within the Gallery app. Which album it's saved into depends on the size, type and origin of the photo or video. Most of the time you'll find your files stored in the Camera and Video folders, but occasionally you might find them in similar albums. Many third-party apps will add their own unique albums to the Gallery app. An example of this is WhatsApp, which adds its own album for all the photos that are sent to you through the messaging platform. The way your albums are arranged is very straightforward. All of your albums are arranged in a list down the left side of the screen that lets you quickly hop between different folders and by tapping on an album the contents will be displayed to the right. The other screen furniture includes icons to create new albums, launch the Camera app and access a menu of other

features that let you select photos, delete photos, view an album as a slideshow, access the Settings and visit the brilliant Studio, whereby you can start getting really creative with your photos.

Sort your photos

If you're a keen photo hoarder then being able to sort through your photos will be of vital importance. Luckily for Galaxy users, the Gallery app includes a series of sorting options that you can access by tapping the icon in the top-left corner. By default your photos will be stored inside albums, but this can be changed so that your photos are stored in chronological order, by subject matter, or even by the people who were tagged in them. The Scenery view is a brilliant way to see exactly where your holiday snaps were shot.

Organise your photos

If you're not happy with where some of your photos are being stored then don't worry, as the Gallery app is highly customisable. Each photo can be renamed, moved and deleted to keep all your albums organised. Moving said photos is an easy enough process; all that's required is a long-press on the photo in question to enable the tickbox selection process, and then tapping the menu icon to select a place to move them to. After a few minutes of sorting out the contents of your Gallery app, you'll have a much more organised app that you can use without worrying it'll get cluttered.

You may want to tweak the colours of your images a little, add some fun effects to them or even scribble notes on them. You can do all of this with Gallery's partner app, Studio. Simply hit the menu icon while viewing an image and select Studio. You can also open an image and tap the Edit icon to start making tweaks.

Make artistic adjustments and then share your edited photos directly to Facebook and Twitter

View a slideshow

1 Starter image Open an album and then select the first image of your slideshow.

2 Choose Slideshow Press the Menu button, then select Slideshow from the list.

3 Settings The slideshow will start to play but you can tap the screen to change the settings.

4 Tweak settings Here you can apply filters, music and more to make your show captivating.

Story Album

Save your favourite photo memories into completely customisable photo albums with Story Album

You'll use it to…

Arrange your images
Lay out your photos however you like

Add a theme
Choose from a wide variety of different album layouts

Tell a story
Add captions and maps to your albums

Customise layouts
Modify, resize, crop and arrange your photos to suit your needs

Share with friends
Publish your story albums online

Print your story
Print a physical book of your story album

Fig 1 (right) Select a theme that fits with the type of images you're using

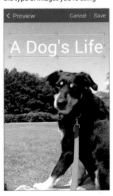

Fig 2 (above) Story Album places your images into an interactive photo album

Exhibit your favourite photos

With Samsung's Story Album app you can import and arrange all of your favourite images from your Galaxy device into a comprehensive photo album. By combining photos, captions, maps and titles you'll be able to compile a scrapbook of memories using one of the app's beautifully designed themes to present your images exactly how you like.

Create a new album

To create a Story album open the app and tap the '+' icon in the top right corner of the screen. Tap Gallery albums and you'll be directed to the Galleries app where you'll be able to select the images that you want to include in your album. You'll also be able to add or remove images at any point when editing your album. Tap on images to select them then tap Done. In the album creation window you can add a title and cover image to your album. Tap on the menu icon in the top-right corner and then choose the Edit cover option. Tap on the default image to choose from any of the images that you've imported from Galleries as your cover image. Tap on Theme to explore Story Album's available themes. Each theme has its own unique style, presenting your images in different arrangements and frames. Once you've picked a title, theme and cover image tap Create album and all of your selected images will be compiled into the album. With an album open tap the menu button to edit your title, cover image or theme as well as add new images and content to your Story Album.

Edit an album

Add more content
As mentioned before it's possible to add content other than images to your albums. Tap the menu button then tap Add content. Form here you can connect to the appropriate app to add a location (Google Maps) or text (S Memo). Once you've input location details on Google Maps or text into S Memo it will be added to your album. Tapping on a map or text element in Story Album will allow you to edit it. Tap the menu button and tap Remove Content to extract an element from the selected album page, replacing it with another image.

1 Edit Mode Press and hold on any artefact within an album to enter edit mode.

2 Move item Press and hold on an image then drag it to reposition it.

Share your Story Album
Once you've completed an album then it's time to start sharing it. Select one of your albums from the Story Album main menu and tap the share button. There are multiple sharing options. Firstly you can tap Share via to send the album as an image file, PDF or a Story Album file (.scc) to people. Select a format you want to send the album as then choose what app you want to share it via, such as Gmail or ChatON. Keep in mind only those who have the Story Album app will be able to view .scc files. Tap Export from the Story Album menu to create a PDF or .scc file which will be stored on your device. Tap Print to print the album using a Wi-Fi connected printer, or tap Order Photo Book to order a physical copy.

3 Tool bar Use the Tool bar to rotate images, rearrange the page and remove images.

Story Album can suggest albums to be created by analysing images in the Gallery app

4 Resizing Pinch and drag inwards/outwards on an image to resize it within its frame.

Kindle for Samsung

Download your favourite books and read them on your Galaxy using Kindle for Samsung

You'll use it to…

Browse for books
Choose from over one million books

Subscribe
Receive issues of your favourite magazines

Sync across multiple devices
Start exactly where you left off on any Samsung device

Interact with a book
Make notes, highlight and look up words in books

Download free books
Get a free book once a month with your Samsung account

Build a library
Manage and categorise your favourite reads

Read on your Galaxy

The Kindle for Samsung app was built exclusively for Samsung devices. It offers all of the great features that come with the standard Kindle Android App with the added bonus of being formatted for your Galaxy, making the app easier to navigate, use and read from. Samsung users are also given a free download every month.

Getting started

You can download the Kindle for Samsung app from Galaxy Apps. On opening the app tap Start Reading. You'll be asked

Fig 1 (right) Read and buy books on your Galaxy with Amazon's Kindle app

Fig 2 (above) Download a free Kindle Book on your Samsung Galaxy device

to login to your Amazon account. If you don't have one tap Create an account. Once signed in you'll be taken to the home page. Any books you have previously purchased through Amazon will be added to the app automatically. Just swipe through your library and tap on a book to download and read it. Tap the menu button in the top-left. Under the Store heading tap Samsung Book Deals. You'll be prompted to sign into your Samsung account. Once signed in you can return to the Samsung Book Deals page to view the books, which are now available for free. Samsung users can download one book per month from the available collection without charge. From the selection tap on the book's front cover to visit its details page. From here you can read a synopsis and product details, check out customer reviews or share the book's details page through another app. If happy with your choice tap Buy Now with 1-click and the book will be added to your Kindle for Samsung Library.

Browse the Kindle Store

Tap the Shopping cart icon at the top right hand corner of the app to access the Kindle Store. Store items are broken into three subsections. Kindle ebooks, Kindle magazines & Journals and Kindle Newspapers. Tap on a category to begin browsing or use the search tool. Some Magazines or Newspapers can be subscribed to, and a separate button for Subscribing will appear on the items details page. You'll need to have a payment method setup on your Amazon account to buy books. This can be done from a computer by logging into **amazon.co.uk** or an Amazon App.

Build a digital library

From the menu button tap All items to see all of your purchased books. Tap and hold on a book thumbnail to display the book's options menu. Here you can Remove the book from your device and manage the download in many other ways. Tap Add to collection. Title your new collection, tap Create then tap OK. Repeat this step for however many books you like. From the apps menu under the Library Subheading tap Collections to view and modify your existing collections. Collections are a great way to manage and order your own personal library of digital literature.

Books not downloaded to your Galaxy can be accessed from the Cloud tab on your library

Navigate books

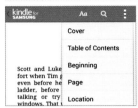

1 **Navigation** Tap on a page then tap the options button. Tap Go To, to navigate around the book.

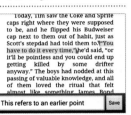

2 **Add notes** Tap and hold on a piece of text to select it. Tap Note to add notes to the page.

3 **Search** With text selected tap More to search for the selection in the book or on the web.

4 **Dictionary** When making a selection tap Download to download the dictionary add-on.

Kindle for Samsung

Fig 3 (above) Amazon will recommend other authors and books based upon your reading history

Get recommendations on ebooks

One of the best things about the Kindle app for Samsung is that it's constantly adding new and engaging titles across all genres to provide the most thorough ebook storefront around. After prolonged use, you'll notice some gradual change in how the app works for you. You'll see lots of recommendations appearing through several menus accessible from the home page of the app. Scroll to the bottom of the app and eventually you'll find a recommended list based on your previous purchases. The app will also give you recommendations based on specified authors that you access often; again this is all available through the home page after prolonged use. The other ways users can get recommendations through the Kindle for Samsung app is by

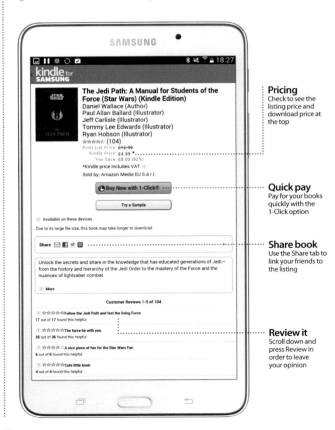

Pricing
Check to see the listing price and download price at the top

Quick pay
Pay for your books quickly with the 1-Click option

Share book
Use the Share tab to link your friends to the listing

Review it
Scroll down and press Review in order to leave your opinion

Fig 4 (above) Download a book on to your Samsung before reading

If you're ever lost within the Kindle app, make sure to take advantage of the superb side menu

How to buy a book

1 Choose book Use the Kindle Store and search function to find a book you want to purchase.

reading reviews on each dedicated ebook's page. All reviews are stored at the bottom of each page and will help you figure out if a book is worth a download, or best worth avoiding. If you have several friends who also use the Kindle app, then they can also send you links and recommended reads, which you can open up and look at on your Galaxy device.

2 Sample Before buying, use the Try it Out tab to read a sample of the book for free.

Reading your ebooks

After you've put together a list of ebooks, you can begin reading them. Amazon is famed for its simple Kindle reading software and the app includes many great features that make it a decent e-reader. First and foremost you'll need to download the book onto your Galaxy, before flicking through pages of the book using your volume keys. By pressing on a particular page, you can then change things like the font size, colour, or simply highlight a word that you don't understand. On newer Samsung Galaxy devices, you'll be able to use the bookmark feature. As its name suggests, this will create a virtual bookmark so that you can come back to the correct spot later. Once you're finished with the book, you can choose to remove it from your device to help save on internal storage.

3 Login Go back to the book's screen and press the 1-Click tab and log in to your account.

Get free and exclusive books

1 Book deals Open the Samsung Book Deals page through the side menu to claim your free book.

2 Make a choice You'll have a choice between four books per month; just select the one you want.

4 Payment Choose an existing payment or add a new one before confirming the purchase.

Samsung Music

Samsung Music

Use the music player app to play your favourite songs on the move

You'll use it to...

Play music
Load music onto your Tab and listen to it while on the move

Control track order
Modify the order you play tracks via shuffle, repeat and more

Make playlists
Create your own personal jukebox

Import music
Import your tunes via USB

Get info
Search online for more information about your favourite songs

Tweak sound
Change the equaliser settings

Fig 1 (right) You can shuffle tracks, toggle playing order and even create your own playlists in the playback screen

Fig 2 (above) Pull down the notification panel to reveal playback controls

Listening to music

Listening to your favourite music is simple on your Galaxy device as it features a cool little music-playing app with a simple control set to enable you to find what you want to listen to quickly and then play it effortlessly (Fig 1). To access it, tap on the Samsung Music app, which in turn will reveal your music files. Browse your music library and then tap on a track to start playing it. If you happen to be on a home screen then you can access a simple set of playback controls to manage your music by swiping down from the top of the screen to access your notifications panel (Fig 2).

Browse your library

If you currently have a gamut of music files on your Samsung Galaxy then you can, with the aid of Samsung Music, organise them into a library of songs. When you launch Samsung Music you can use the tabs at the top of the interface to locate your music files. The Tracks tab will list all of your songs alphabetically and, moving to the right of the same menu bar, tap on Albums to group all of your songs into their respective albums or instead tap on Artists to list all of the tracks by the artist or band who performed them. You can swipe all the way to the far right in order to reveal the Folder button. Tapping this allows you to see a basic grouping of your tracks in terms of where they're stored. This option is ideal if you want to group different music formats and styles together.

The MP3 is no longer the only popular format out there either. Extra memory (the Galaxy S7's 32GB of storage can be expanded massively with Micro SD memory cards) means that FLAC and WAV-format music files are numerous and common nowadays.

Master playback controls

Playing music provides many additional interface options. The base of the screen shows the basic Play/Pause button in the centre and the Forward and Backward buttons to skip tracks on either side. Tap the track name to be taken to a new play screen showcasing the album sleeve art and plenty more options besides. Swipe the artwork left and right to skip tracks, press the icon just underneath to the left to shuffle tracks, the icon to the right of that repeats one or more tracks. The interface is simple and accessible to every music fan, and ideal for quickly finding the songs you want to hear.

Create playlists

To access a playlist, swipe through the options at the top of the screen until you come to Playlists. If you wish to create a new playlist, tap on the '+' icon at the bottom of the screen next to the 'Create Playlist' header. A new box will then appear on the screen. Enter a catchy title for your new playlist and tap Create. Now you need to start choosing tracks to add. Tick the box to select a track and then tap Done when you have finished.

When selecting files for a new playlist, tick the box in the top corner to select all of your music

Set the equaliser

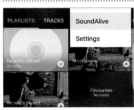

1 **EQ button** Tap on the More option in the top-right corner and choose 'SoundAlive'.

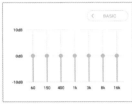

2 **Basic EQ** A basic EQ will be displayed that you can customise to suit your needs.

3 **Custom EQ** Tap on the Custom option to bring up a list of presets for music styles.

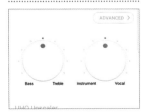

4 **Advanced controls** Tap on the 'Basic' option to bring up a more advanced control set.

Samsung Music

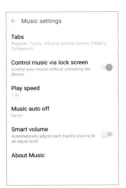

← Music settings

Tabs
Playlists, Tracks, Albums, Artists, Genres, Folders, Composers

Control music via lock screen
Control your music without unlocking the device.

Play speed
1.0x

Music auto off
Never

Smart volume
Automatically adjust each track's volume to an equal level.

About Music

Fig 3 (above) Access the app settings to tweak certain aspects…

Explore the settings

You can access the settings (Fig 3) for the Samsung Galaxy app by tapping on the More option in the top-right corner of the interface. The First option in settings lets you edit which tabs are displayed across the top of the screen. You can tick or untick the boxes next to each category to determine what is displayed and adjust the order in which they are presented across the top of the screen by pressing and holding on the arrow icons and moving them up or down. The next option should be turned on by default, but if you don't wish to access your music controls from your lock screen then you can turn the option off.

Other options within the app settings let you adjust the play speed and enable Smart Volume to play each track at the same

Menu bar
The main menu options for Samsung Music provide the majority of settings and tweaks

Main screen
Your music tracks are listed here, Just tap to play each one and you will be able to control them

Index
An alphabetical search list runs vertically down the right side of the screen. Tap or drag here to quickly scroll the list of tracks

Play controls
The main music controls are listed at the bottom of the screen. The EQ buttons is also here

To delete a song, tap on the More button, choose Edit and then pick songs to remove

level. Finally, if you like to listen to your music while going to sleep, for example, then you can use the 'Music auto off' option to stop your music after a determined length of time. Tap this option to determine the time before your music stops playing.

Import more tunes

To import tunes via USB, plug the supplied cable into your Galaxy and connect the other end to a computer housing your music archive. Make sure download and launch the SmartSwitch app for your Mac or PC (go to **www.samsung.com/uk/smart-switch**) and then when you connect your device to your computer using the USB cable you will get a message on your device prompting you to allow access to device data. Select 'Allow' and you're all set. You can even monitor the connection process through the SmartSwitch app on your computer.

Once connected, click on the downward arrow next to your device name and click on the folder icon next to the Internal Memory option. Now navigate your way to the Music folder on your device and drag and drop music files from your computer into this destination to copy them across.

Queue the music

1 Tap Queue On the main playback screen, tap the 'Queue' option in the top-right corner.

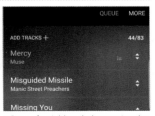

2 Set order Add tracks by tapping the '+' icon and adjust the running order by holding the arrows.

Get song info

1 Tap More While playing a song, tap on the 'More' option in the top-right corner.

2 Song details Now select the 'Details' option from the menu that appears…

3 View details Information about the song currently playing will then be displayed.

4 Search online Tap the 'Search Online' option and pick a service to find out more.

Video Player

You can play a wide variety of videos on your
Samsung Galaxy device

You'll use it to…

Play movies
Watch a video file on your Tab

Edit videos
Trim your home video clips

Tag friends
Identify the people in your videos

Send via Bluetooth
Connect to other Bluetooth devices

Float videos on-screen
Use the Pop up play option

Upload videos
Share your clips on YouTube

Watching videos

You have the ability to not
only play a range of videos
that are currently stored on
your Samsung Galaxy device,
but you can also choose to
manipulate them in a variety
of ways, such as tagging
people who appear inside
them or even trimming clips
down to focus on the main
action without having to
leave the Video app. You can
also share your videos via
other devices and apps, or
upload them to the internet.

Play a file

Playing a video file on
the Samsung Galaxy is
straightforward, and the
Video app will appear to be
quite similar to many other devices playing the same sort of media,
albeit with a few tweaks relating to the particular platform, of course
(Fig 1). To begin, enter your App Drawer and tap on Video, which
will then open up the app and display the files. Decide on how you
would like the files to be displayed by tapping the menu icon in the
top-right corner and choosing 'View as'. Now pick a display option
from Grid view, List view or Folder view (Fig 2). Once you have
scanned the list of files that are available, tap on the one that you
want to watch. As soon as you initiate the file, it will load and then
begin to play automatically.

Fig 1 (right) Video Player makes great use of
your Samsung Galaxy's powerful hardware

Fig 2 (above) Videos can be catalogued as
animated thumbnails. Tap to play one

Depending on the format of the video, you may need to rotate your device in order to view the video at the correct aspect ratio. If the playback controls are hidden from view (they tend to move out of your way, giving you more screen real estate to enjoy the video with, after a few seconds), just tap on the screen to display them again. Press Pause and Play alternately to stop and start the film, and skip forwards and backwards to view other video files. Once the video begins to play, the controls will disappear again.

Tweak playback options

While you are playing a video, tap on the Menu button on your Galaxy and a new pop-up menu will appear. Select Settings and tap the Play Speed option, and you can then increase the speed at which the video plays so it is up to 1.5 times faster or instead lower it to a minimum of 0.5X, which is half speed. If the files are available on your device (usually .srt files) then you can also switch on subtitles, and you can also get your Galaxy to automatically play the next video file in the line-up to save you manually selecting it. Also, from the Menu button, tap Chapter preview to jump to specific points.

Shoot and tag videos

Of course, on a Samsung Galaxy, videos can also be shot as well as viewed, although in this case the Video app must be placed to one side for the moment as the Camera app comes back into play. To shoot and tag your videos, open up the Camera app and then tap to enter the Settings section at the top-left of the screen. Scroll down the menu until you reach the GPS tag section. After tapping this, a small window will appear on the screen. Tap on it and the videos you shoot will now be tagged.

To select content to play from your Dropbox account, tap the menu icon and choose it

Use Pop up play

1 Choose video Open the Video Player app and choose the video you would like to play.

2 Play video Tap on your chosen video file and it will then appear on-screen and start playing.

3 Pop-up Tap on the small Pop up play icon in order to start the function.

4 Move window Move the Pop up play window around the screen to work around it.

The apps

Fig 3 (above) Connect, or 'pair', with
another device to send data via Bluetooth

Video Player

Connect to Bluetooth devices scanning and sharing

Sharing files has become almost second nature to users of Samsung Galaxy devices – sharing a video via email, MMS or via social sites such as Facebook is relatively common. You can choose to go direct, however, and share it via Bluetooth – that is, transfer data from one particular device to another. To do so, you will need to switch on Bluetooth, which can be done by entering Settings from the home screen. Under the Quick Settings section at the top is the Bluetooth option. Flick the switch to On and the tiny Bluetooth icon will appear at the very top of your screen. Now, you will need to connect to a device to share data, so tap on Bluetooth beside the switch and then Scan at the bottom of the next screen. When a device is found, it will be listed under Available devices. Tap one to

Top menu
The menu at the top of the screen allows you to decide how you will view the video content on your Galaxy device

Thumbnails
In thumbnail view, the images for each video are animated, giving you a preview of the content

Video title
The text situated next to the file, is the file name of that video

Running time
Underneath the title is the total running time. Before that is the current position in the video

Before you post your video to YouTube, tap on Privacy so you can limit who is able to view it

Trim video clips

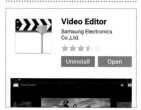

'pair', or connect, then follow the confirmation request that appears. Now, return to the Video app, find and play your selected video, tap on the share icon at the top, select Bluetooth and tap your paired device; the video will be sent directly to it.

1 Get software Start off by downloading the Video Editor app from Galaxy Apps.

Upload to YouTube

It is possible to share your video with many different devices and services, but posting to YouTube is slightly different because, by doing it this way, you are allowing the general public to view your work instead of an individual or a select group of people. The process of uploading to YouTube is, on the face of it, similar to sharing data with other services. Hence, you open up Video Player and select your video, and then tap on the Menu button to examine the options. Near the top of the menu is the Share via feature, which you can tap to enter a full screen of possible destinations. This is where you can select YouTube. Tap YouTube, and then enter the title of the video you want to upload, a description, tags and, indeed, whether or not you want to make it public. Then tap the upload key – which is the up arrow at the top of the screen – in order to send the video to YouTube.

2 Open in Video In the Video app, select a video, tap the menu icon and choose Edit.

3 Trim In Video Editor, tap on the video and then move the frame around the video to trim it.

Select multiple videos for upload

4 Confirm Trim Tap the Done icon, and the new parameters will be saved.

1 Select Share To share multiple videos at once press and hold on any video and then tick them.

2 Select video Now tap the menu icon, choose the Share Via option and then pick a means to share.

Kids Mode

Kids Mode

Samsung's Kids Mode allows you to control which apps your children can use via an intuitive interface

You'll use it to...

Protect the settings on a Tab
Stop children accidentally wiping the device

Track the device usage
Understand how much time is spent on the tablet

Set daily usage limits
Control your children's access to the device and easily ensure use is not excessive

Limit approved media
Ensure kids see only appropriate content

Keep children safe
Ensure they only use content that you approve of

Installing Kids Mode

Some Galaxy devices don't have Kids Mode installed by default, instead they have a shortcut which redirects to Galaxy Apps. Click the icon you'll be presented with a download option. If the shortcut is not included, try adding a widget to your home screen and see if 'Kids Mode 1x1' appears. If it does, add this to your home screen and click to download and install the main app.

Explore the features

The Kids Mode application uses large, bright icons that are attractive to children, together with an intuitive user interface and built-in applications. There is also a 'Kids Store' section; this includes both free and paid Samsung and third-party applications for Kids Mode for additional functionality. Kids Mode already includes a drawing and colouring application in which children can either draw their own pictures with a number of brushes or they can use one of a large number of stickers before saving their creations to view in the gallery. A sound recording tool allows children to alter the sound of their voice to match on-screen characters and a camera app enables them to take pictures or videos. Access and usage limits can be controlled individually.

Fig 1 (above right) Access to features in Kids Mode can be adjusted to suit each user's age

Fig 2 (above) After the introduction screens, familiarise yourself with the Kids Mode features

Adding your movies

Kids Mode includes a media player, allowing you to load kid-friendly movies onto your device. This too is subject to usage limits if you have defined them. Internal storage is limited but microSD cards of up to 128GB are available on some devices, so to ensure that the device continues to run smoothly it's best to put movies on the card. This also makes copying the files across from a PC easier. Videos can be approved per item, allowing you to have multiple videos on a card and allow access to them individually.

Change authorised applications

Within Kids Mode, it is possible to add applications that are downloaded via the Play Store or Samsung Apps in addition to the purpose-built apps that can be installed from the Kids Mode store. By default, all non-Kids Mode apps are disabled, so a parent needs to log in (by entering the secure PIN) and authorise each app individually. Although authorised apps effectively launch outside of the Kids Mode app, children are still unable to break out of the limited environment, because if they close the app or press the home button, they will be returned back to the Kids Mode interface. Configuration of the authorised applications can be found in the parental control menu, which is accessed using the 'hand-holding icon' in the bottom right. When adding third-party apps, it's important to remember that they're adapted for children, so you should ensure that the content is appropriate and particularly that they don't allow the child to break out of the 'walled garden' of Kids Mode via access to built-in web browsers, app launchers or similar. You should also be aware that when applications are automatically updated they will remain accessible from within Kids Mode.

Within Kids Mode, you can customise your child's profile; multiple children can have an account

More Kids Mode tips

1 Playful crocodile Your children can interact with the crocodile and the vibrant scenery.

2 Using gifts Authorised apps first appear to your children as gifts that they can click to reveal.

3 Launching Kids Mode be found in the application launcher, and can be added to the desktop.

4 Exiting A 'door' in the bottom right is used to exit. It's PIN protected for restricted access.

Group Play

Play games, and share videos, photos and more
with friends over multiple devices with Group Play

You'll use it to…

Share content quickly
Share photos, videos and music

Challenge friends
Play multiplayer games

Share documents
Send files to users

Doodle over photos
Edit photos with friends

Connect multiple devices
Link up to five devices

Invite who you like
Create private groups for friends

Fig 1 (right) Newly created Groups in
Group Play can be accessed instantly

Fig 2 (above) Connect with local
friends or users in other countries

Share and play with friends

Group Play from Samsung is a great app for connecting with other Samsung users, regardless of whether you have a Wi-Fi or 3G/4G connection. This is possible through the use of Wi-Fi direct, which can create a closed off connection between multiple devices, allowing you to transfer data and share content with ease.

Host a group play session

To start your Group Play session so you can connect with another device, open the Group Play app. The start window is split into two sections: Join Group, which

displays any groups available to access and Create group which allows you to create your own group. As soon as another Group Play user creates a Group it will appear in this window. Tap on the Group name to join it. For more joining options tap the options button at the top right of the window and tap settings. Here you can edit your Group Play nickname and decide who can send you invitations. Nearby Friend invitations will connect you with each other via a Wi-Fi direct connection, whereas you will connect with remote friends via a Wi-Fi or 3G/4G connection. When creating a group tap the pencil icon next to the group name to edit it. Tick Set Group password if you would like to secure group access then tap Create. You will be prompted to input a Group Play passcode. Tap OK and you will be taken to your new Group Play session. Other Group Play users within close range will be able to join your session. You will receive a notification whenever someone new joins your session. Now you can share and play together in Group Play.

What Group Play can do

Once you have started a Group Play session and another user has joined, tap on the person icon next to the options button to see which users are active in the session. The model of Galaxy you and the other user have will determine what functions are available in Group Play. Group Camcorder, which allows you to view live camera feeds off other users' devices, is not available on all Samsung devices. All Galaxy smartphones and tablets will allow you to share music, images, videos and documents, and play games with other users in Group Play

How Wi-Fi Direct works

Whichever device is hosting the Group Play session will create a Wi-Fi Direct signal. Other devices can connect to this signal in the same way that you would connect your Galaxy to a Wi-Fi connection. This is the reason why you can use Group Play without a Wi-Fi or 3G/4G connection, because the connection is coming from the hosting device itself. However this does mean that whilst you're connected to a Group Play session via Wi-Fi direct you won't be connected to a normal Wi-Fi connection, you'll have to leave Group Play to reconnect to the internet.

When sending files to another user's device you can access any folder structure on your Galaxy

Video over two screens

1 Share video In Group Play tap Share Video. Select a video file to share then tap Done.

2 Playback Once another device has opened it, tap the screen to display playback options.

3 Multi-screen In the top tool bar press and drag the slider to the multiple device icon.

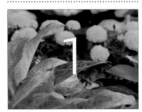

4 Split video The video will be split into two, dividing itself up across the multiple devices.

Group Play

Fig 3 (above) Send your favourite photos
with handwritten notes to friends

Share content in Group Play

In the Group Play session window under the My Apps tab you will find available sharing options. Tap on Share Images. You will be connected to the Galleries app where you can browse through your device's images. Tap the menu icon in the top-right corner of the window to view images by Time or Album. Tap on the image you want to share or Select all to import all of the images from your current gallery into the Group Play session. When happy with your selection tap Done. A person icon will appear next to the Share Images button in any other user's Group Play app who are currently linked to your session. When a Group Play user taps Share Images they will instantly be taken to the photo that you just shared. When viewing shared images, tap the options button then tap Save to

Save files
Tap the option button to Save files or remove them from Group play

Private mode
Private mode lets you remove shared content from a group

Add more
Tap here to add more content to the viewing window

Doodling
Use the doodle tool to add annotations to a document or image

Once a Wi-Fi Direct connection has been made open the Wi-Fi networks to connect to it

save it to your device. From the top tool bar tap the Draw icon to enter drawing mode. Here all users who are sharing the image can doodle over it. Tap the plus icon to add more images. Each sharing tool has different options available within it. When sharing files you will be able to collaborate on the same document, and when sharing videos you can control play back across multiple devices.

More features in Group Play

On top of being able to share content in Group Play you can play games as well. In the Group Play window tap Store. Here you can view all available games and tools that can be downloaded and installed into your Group Play app. There are a variety of different add-ons available, ranging from photo tools, which allow advanced sharing and editing of images in Group Play to multiplayer games like Multi Air Hockey. Note that some add-ons are paid. Tap on an add-on then OK to begin the installation. You will be connected to Galaxy Apps where you can view more details on the add-on. Tap install to install the app to your device. After installation is complete you will find the add-on in your Group Play home screen. Open the add-on and start interacting with other users.

Group Play with remote users

1 Remote sharing With a file selected tap the phone icon to send a remote invitation to one of your contacts.

2 Select a contact Choose a contact. A remote invitation to join the Group Play session will be sent to them.

Stereo speakers

1 Share a track In Group Play's My Apps window tap Share Music. Select a track. Tap Done.

2 Second speaker On another device open the track, turning the device into a speaker.

3 Speaker setup In the tool bar drag the slider toward the cog icon, then tap a speaker.

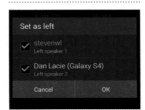

4 Assign speakers Choose which speaker to assign to each device then play the track.

Chromecast

Stream videos from your Samsung Galaxy with Google's innovative Chromecast streaming device

You'll use it to…

Stream videos
Stream stored videos from your device

Work from home
Get documents and more on the big screen

Browse the web
Cast a tab and enjoy browsing

Play games
Choose from a series of Chromecast games

Sync files
Manage files between devices

Look at photos
Share your favourite images on your TV

Fig 1 (right) Once you've set your Chromecast up, you're ready to stream

Fig 2 (above) You can stream from any page with the Cast icon

Get to know Chromecast

Chromecast is a tiny HDMI device that plugs directly into your TV to provide a platform where users can send videos, files and more directly to their TV from their Samsung Galaxy device. It's cheap to purchase and can also be set up in just a few simple steps. Once done, you're ready to explore various streaming options.

Stream with Chromecast

Although Chromecast can link with a ton of apps for added functionality, which

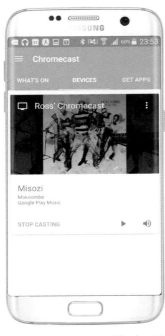

we'll explore later, at its core is a superb streaming suite. Whether it's downloaded videos, or videos captured using your Galaxy device's camera, these can be streamed to Chromecast to appear directly on your TV. Go into the Gallery app on your device and select a locally stored video on it. If you've set up the Chromecast correctly, you should now see a small rectangle symbol on the right of your screen. This icon represents the Cast feature, which is used to send the video across to your TV. Press on the icon and your video will now be shown on your TV to enjoy. Similarly, the Netflix app – a staple for those wanting movies on demand – is compatible with Chromecast. Simply load the movie of your choice and look for

Chromecast

the Cast icon before sending it on to your TV. Many of the movie-based apps on Galaxy Apps and Google Play are compatible with Chromecast, so your best bet is to download some and simply look around for the trusted Cast icon. Once you're finished casting the video on your TV, just press the Cast icon again and the stream will stop, with the video then loading on your Galaxy device.

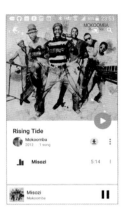

Cast your tunes

Another area in which the Chromecast service works a treat is with streaming music. The predominant app you can use for this is Google Play music, which includes a Cast icon at the top of the Play Music app. Any song can be sent across to your TV and users can even create playlists of songs to stream. Once you've sent a song across, your Samsung Galaxy will be turned into a virtual remote, where you can control volume levels and skip through certain songs. Even better, you can stream podcasts and live music feeds through a wealth of apps available for all Galaxy users.

Working from home

If you're looking for a solution to working from home, Chromecast has it covered. You can cast files, documents and work projects directly to your TV with a bunch of Chromecast-enabled apps. These include the likes of Google Drive, Dropbox and SugarSync. If you then connect a Bluetooth keyboard and mouse to your Galaxy device, you can work completely on your TV. With all your created documents, you can use any of the compatible cloud storage accounts to save and share your files with fellow work colleagues.

Navigate to the Get Apps tab to find an entire section dedicated to Chromecast apps

The apps

Set up Chromecast

1 **Device** Download and open the Chromecast app, then select Devices from the main menu.

2 **Input name** Add a name to the Chromecast and input Wi-Fi details on the Settings screen.

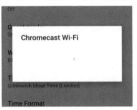

3 **Connect** Your Chromecast will connect to your Wi-Fi and confirm once complete.

4 **Explore** Select Settings from the three-dot menu and edit your device's information.

Maps

Maps

The ideal navigational companion for your
Samsung Galaxy device

You'll use it to…

Find places
Check out locations on a map

Plan routes
Calculate a route from start to finish

Get travel times
See how long it will take by foot, by car or by
public transport

See what's nearby
Find the nearest specialist locations

Navigate
Obtain turn-by-turn directions

Store maps
Save your maps for use offline

Fig 1 (right) It is easy to discover how to get
to a place using Google Maps

Fig 2 (above) Enable the options present in
the Location services settings to enhance
the accuracy of the results

Navigating
with maps

Google's Maps app is
a mature and efficient
navigational tool that takes
full advantage of your
Samsung Galaxy's built-in
GPS system (Fig 1). With GPS,
you can plan a wide number
of routes that will not only
be graphically represented
within the app, but can also
be converted into turn-by-
turn instructions showing
you how to get there.

Find your feet

Maps is an easy-to-use
and efficient app that
will routinely undertake a
number of location-related
tasks, such as devising routes from A to B and finding useful
and important locations in your area or further afield. To do this,
however, the app – and by extension your Samsung Galaxy device
– has to be able to know where you are in the world, which it does
by utilising the GPS system that comes as part of your Galaxy device.
When you buy the phone, this feature will be set to Off by default.
Hence, you naturally have to turn it on to get the full use of Google's
Maps facilities.

To get this particular function up and running, go to your home
screen and tap the Menu button, followed by Settings. Scroll down
to the Network Connections section, where you will notice the

Location option. Tap this option and ensure that the switch at the top of the screen is turned on for the location services (Fig 2). In terms of Google and other services that depend on your location, it is wise to try out all three options at some point, as doing this will enhance the accuracy of any results.

Set home location

1 **Access Maps** While in the Maps app, tap on the menu icon in the lower-left corner.

Search for local hotspots
In your area, especially if you live in an urban environment, there will be a number of services and facilities that you can take advantage of – including food-related locations like restaurants or takeaways, pubs, cafes, B&Bs and even guest houses. To take advantage of this information, tap inside the search box at the top of the screen. Entering keywords such as 'restaurants' will display all local eateries on the map and then you can then tap the list icon to view them all in a handy list format.

2 **Sidebar** This will open up the sidebar. From this menu, tap on the Settings option.

3 **Edit home** From the list of options available tap on Edit home or work.

Get turn-by-turn directions
One of the most useful features of Google's Maps app is the turn-by-turn option. This can be a real life-saver, getting you out of many a sticky situation either because you need to find an unfamiliar place, you are in an unfamiliar (or even familiar) town or city, or you are simply in a rush and need to know the most direct route to your destination. Alternatively, you could simply be lost, in which case this app can represent the perfect solution. To get turn-by-turn directions, open up the Maps app and tap the Directions icon in the search box at the top of the main app screen. When the new screen appears, input your current and destination locations, then tap on the Start button to switch straight into navigation mode. You'll get 3D directions with voice guidance to your destination.

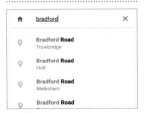

4 **Address** Tap on Home and enter a new address in the search box.

On the Navigation screen, tap on the blue start button to switch straight into navigation mode

Maps

Fig 3 (above) Access commonly needed services through the Services option

Finding services

One of the most interesting features in the most recent version of Google Maps is the way it is set up to provide you with the most relevant information at any given time. This is seen most effectively within the Services feature, which delivers instant access to a wealth of commonly used services that you'll need while on the road, such as petrol stations, cashpoints or taxi ranks. You access Services by tapping into the search box from the main map screen (Fig 3). A short scroll down reveals the Services option, with four icons representing the ones you most frequently use (tapping 'view more categories' will reveal many more). Tapping on any of the icons will take you back to the map screen with each of the available services in that category marked on the map. The name of the service is

Search box
Either search for an address or tap the empty box for context-sensitive information

Main menu
Tap here to access the various map options and settings available

Main screen
This large area is where you can view your map. Pan and zoom with gesture controls

Current location
The compass point here at the bottom right can be tapped to return you to your current location

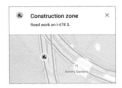

A road sign icon appears on the map with guidance on how this will affect your travel plans

detailed at the bottom of the screen, and swiping left and right will take you through all of the results, while simultaneously highlighting their position on the map. Tapping the List icon that appears in the search box gives you all the results in list form, ordered by proximity.

Traffic and transport

Google Maps has long had support for live traffic information, and this has been further developed in the latest version of the app. From the main map screen tap on the list icon in the top-left corner to access the menu. The first option on the list is Traffic. Tapping this adds live traffic information to the map, with colour coding on major roads: green shows traffic flowing normally, yellow suggests heavy traffic but no delays, and red indicates delays. Traffic incidents are also reported. A road sign icon appears on the map, and tapping it opens a pop-up window revealing the nature of the incident as well as guidance on how this will affect your travel plans. If you're not driving you can also access public transport information within the app. Open the sidebar once again and select the second option. You'll now see routes and stations for various types of transport as well as, in supported regions, schedule information.

Use offline maps

1 Find the option Tap inside the empty search box from the main screen and scroll down.

2 Save the map Tap Make this map area available offline and your map view will be downloaded.

Different map views

1 Traffic Real time traffic conditions are displayed as an overlay on main roads.

2 Transport Public transport routes are shown in regions where they are supported.

3 Cycling You can view cycle routes to determine off-road routes to your destination.

4 Satellite Google Maps' famed satellite view is also supported with high-res imagery.

Google Drive

Discover how Google's versatile cloud storage service will revolutionise the way in which you work

You'll use it to…

Store files
Keep your important files safe in one place

Access from anywhere
Access your Drive from any mobile device or computer

Collaborate
Work on projects with other people

Stay organised
Create folders to keep all of your files neatly organised

Work offline
Download files to your device to carry on working on the move

Scan docs
Use your Galaxy's camera to photograph and store files as PDFs

Fig 1 (right) Tapping on the three-dot icon lets you manage and view your content in a variety of ways…

Fig 2 (above) The 'i' icon lets brings up a wealth of options regarding the select file

Store files online

Google Drive is a useful and versatile cloud storage service that makes it easy to store files and access them from any device, anywhere in the world. If the app doesn't come pre-installed on your Galaxy device, then you can download it for free from the Google Play Store and, once installed, it will be added to the means by which you can share files from your device.

Easy interface

By default, your Google Drive account comes with a staggering 15GB of free storage space and an intuitive interface that makes it easy to view and manage all of the content that you upload either by list or by grid view, which you can toggle by tapping the icon in the top-right corner of the screen. Tapping on the three-dot icon will also provide ways to sort and filter your content (Fig 1) and this, coupled with a smart search engine means that you'll always be able to find the files that you need quickly and easily.

Google Drive works seamlessly with other Google services, such as Gmail and Google+ Photos, so you can store files, save email attachments and back-up photos directly to the service. What's more, Drive makes working remotely from the office easy thanks to the way it is integrated into Google's suite of office apps, such as Docs, Sheets and Slides. As such you can create new documents on your device and then effortlessly beam them into the office and even collaborate on live projects with other people.

Uploading files

There are two ways to upload files to Google Drive. You can tap the Share button from within any other app and choose the Drive option from the list of possible options. Alternatively, tap on the red '+' icon while in the app and start the upload process there. Tapping the '+' icon brings up plenty of other options. You can create a new folder, create new files for Docs, Sheets or Slides and even scan. The latter lets you take a photo of documents and upload them to Drive as PDFs.

The upload process is a lot more efficient if you are connected to Wi-Fi, as uploading files on a mobile data plan may incur additional costs. On the flip-side, if you know that you aren't going to have access to Wi-Fi, you can make files available offline so that you can view them when your device loses service. Simply tap on the small 'i' icon next to the document to bring up the info page and move the 'Keep on device' slider to 'On'.

Sharing files

As we mentioned, tapping the 'i' icon next to a document will bring up the option to keep a version on your device, but there are plenty of other options available via the info page too (Fig 2). It is here that you can add people to collaborate on the file, share a link, mark the file with a star to make it easier to find, move the file to a different location, send the file to other people, download it to your device and rename it. Scroll down the page further and you will be able to set sharing permissions and see who currently has access to the file.

To find files easily, mark them with a star, tap the menu, select 'Starred' and marked files will be listed

Uploading files

1 Tap the '+' To upload, tap on the '+' icon in the lower-right corner of the Drive interface.

2 Choose Upload From the menu that appears, choose the 'Upload' option to select files.

3 Find file An 'Open from' menu will appear that lets you easily navigate through your files.

4 Upload file Tap a file you wish to upload and it'll be processed and uploaded in minutes.

Google Now

The beauty of Google Now is that it can automate many different areas of your life which can often be time consuming or repetitive

You'll use it to...

Check the weather
See the current weather conditions for multiple locations

Manage your portfolio
Check the prices of the markets and of your stocks

Track your deliveries
Incoming packages are displayed for you to track instantly

See stories of interest
Have web articles automatically delivered to your device

Ask any question
Ask a range of questions based on your personal information

Useful and timely alerts
You will be notified of flight times and other important events

Fig 1 (right) Your location, interests and other data help personalise Google Now

Fig 2 (above) Information is taken from your Gmail account

Make it personal

Google Now requires many permissions to make the experience fit you and your interests. It uses the entirety of the Google services as one to provide timely updates and data based on your current location and activities. It will offer details of events and establishments near to you and can also provide extra information such as travelling directions and opening times. Web articles will be added to the main Google Now interface and will be based on the interests you have specified (Fig 1), and the current and future weather conditions are always on hand when you need them. Google Now can be many things and is completely customisable for your specific needs, and over time it will become even more useful as more information is fed into it. It has the ability to learn about you and work as the perfect personal assistant every single day.

Email updates always on hand

The fact that Google Now is so closely embedded with Gmail is a huge advantage because it takes the functionality of the service to a whole new level. As time passes, you will no doubt receive many emails that require you to create new tasks or add calendar appointments, but with Google Now many of these can be tracked automatically. If you have received order notifications, the parcels will be displayed automatically in Google Now (Fig 2) so that you can track them continually. Statuses of flights you are taking soon are constantly updated and the list continues to cover so many other aspects that would otherwise require manual handling. It can at times feel slightly intrusive, but no individual person is checking through your email, it is done automatically so you can feel safe that your data is only being used for the right reasons. This particular part of Google Now is one that grows more important over time and it will likely give you more reasons to use the service than any other. It is truly revolutionary in so many different ways.

Customise Google Now

1 **The settings** Tap the top-left menu icon to access the full Google Now settings menu.

Find anything instantly

At the top of the Google Now screen is the familiar microphone icon which requires a simple tap to activate. It works exactly like the standard Google search, in that it is quick and accurate, but it is also able to leverage your personal information so that you can undertake urgent searches whenever you need to. For example, if you are travelling to a particular destination and need to know the traffic conditions, just ask and a map will be displayed showing the traffic situation (Fig 3). You can ask what your next appointment is, what the weather will be like tomorrow and almost anything else that comes to mind. The only limit to what Google Now can find is governed by your imagination as it can search for virtually anything you need in an instant.

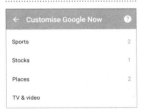

2 **Select Customise** Tap Customise to see the various sections you can change.

3 **Your interests** Add your favourite sports teams in the 'Everything else' section.

4 **Your input** The more specific data you add, the more detailed the information you get will be.

When prompted to specify your preferred units and other info, add it for future efficiency

The apps

S Note

S Note

Use S Note to make both quick sketches and important, complex notes

You'll use it to...

Make notes
If you remember something, keep a record

Capture ideas
If you catch an epiphany, never let it go

Draw diagrams
Make your plans more visual

Turn handwriting into text
Write notes the comfortable way

Send notes to others
Share your thoughts with friends

Group ideas into folders
Bring notes on a single subject together

Fig 1 (right) You can write simple handwritten notes or undertake much more complex tasks with S Note

Fig 2 (above) Use S Note to keep all your ideas organised

Getting ideas down

S Note, or if you don't have it then its sister app S Memo, lets you write or draw notes directly onto the screen of your Galaxy device (Fig 1). You can gather notes together into folders to keep things on similar topics together and also place a home screen widget for quick access (Fig 2). S Note is best used on a Galaxy Note device, where it works in combination with the S Pen stylus in order to allow for fast and easy note-making.

Use S Note's templates

S Note is deceptively easy to use for taking basic notes, yet it is extremely flexible and can be used in lots of different ways. If you start off using it for things like shopping lists, which is what many smartphone-based notes apps are appropriated for, you will soon realise that it has potential way beyond that kind of thing, because it can cope with shapes, formulas, drawings, text and even recorded notes, and since notes can be grouped into folders when shared beyond the app – and beyond the device – the uses are endless. Unfortunately, S Memo is lacking a few of these features.

To start off, run S Note and then tap the + symbol in order to create a new note. You can select a number of templates or just a plain note to work with. Writing text straight onto the screen with your finger or an S Pen is generally the quickest and easiest way to get started, but if you look at the top of the screen then you will also see a range of other options to choose from, including a 'T' symbol that allows you to turn handwriting into text and a shapes symbol that enables you to draw shapes directly onto the screen. In addition to this, you can insert images too.

Handwrite text and use brushes

When writing on the screen, you might at first only feel confident writing ordinary words and sentences. To get past this, it is perhaps important to bear in mind that you can transform your scribing digit into all manner of writing and drawing implements with the aid of in-app pen and brush settings. Tap the pen icon and you will see a range of settings appear on the screen that let you choose different brush types, stroke thicknesses and styles, not to mention ink colours. You can save anything that you particularly like as a preset so that you can use it as often as you like.

Add images to notes

A picture says a thousand words – at least that's what people say, anyway. With S Note, you can combine words and images into a single item, bringing them together in order to help emphasise your point. You can draw in images from the Gallery app, as well as use Maps, a wide range of built-in clip art and shapes, and even videos. Plus, you can record videos and take photos without leaving S Note.

Once you've placed an image onto a note, you can resize it so that it fits your requirements, rotate it, and then apply a range of different effects to make a photo look like as though it has been hand-drawn. The scope to get creative is immense.

You can make use of the sketch effect in order to give your photos that nice hand-drawn look

Inserting shapes

1 Tap menu Tap on the menu icon in the top-right corner and then choose 'Insert'.

2 Choose illustration From the menu that appears, tap on the 'Illustration' option.

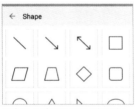

3 Choose shape Now select the 'Shape' option and you will see a wide range of shapes. Pick one.

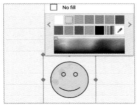

4 Style shape Drag the shape into position and then tap 'Properties' to style it.

S Planner

Use S Planner to manage your time effectively and keep important dates in mind

You'll use it to…

Remember events
Never forget your important dates

Stay organised
Note down tasks to do later

Manage time
Keep track of everything in your life

Total recall
Store all of your great ideas

Plan ahead
View your upcoming schedule

Organising your life

One thing smartphones can do really well is put your diary in your pocket. Your phone is with you all the time, so there's really no reason for not being up to speed with where you need to be and at what time.

Navigate the calendar views

One of the great things about S Planner is the range of different views it lets you have of all the important information you need to keep in a calendar. Using the Samsung Galaxy S6, for example, you've got no fewer

than five different views on offer. You switch between them by tapping the menu icon in the top-right corner of the screen and choosing from Year, Month, Week, Day and Tasks.

Year view (Fig 1) is ideal for looking up dates, and you can tap any month on show to drop straight into Month view (Fig 2). That one displays each day in a grid layout, with text for your commitments on show. If you are a busy person there won't be room to display everything you are up to, but Week view gives you an hour-by-hour breakdown which will show everything you have planned.

Day view gives you the full details on your commitments, and List view shows all your upcoming commitments, not bothering with days when you are free. Agenda view shows your to-do items.

Fig 1 (right) Keep track of the whole year with the S Planner app

Fig 2 (above) The Month view gives you a clear view of your upcoming commitments

Sync calendar accounts

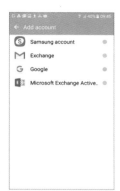

Increasingly, we maintain more than one calendar. You might have a work calendar and a separate one for home. Your significant other might have a calendar that you have access to in order to know when they are busy and free. Keeping track of them all can be irritating.

However, it is possible to view multiple calendars easily. When using S Planner on your Samsung Galaxy, hit the More button and tap Manage Calendars. By tapping Add account you will be able to add a wide range of calendars from various different sources, including Google and Facebook.

Create a new event

The S Planner app lets you store all of your important dates and events, and creating a new calendar event is a quick and easy process thanks to S Planner's intuitive interface. There two ways to create an event – you can either press and hold on the date in question until an event box pops up, or you can tap the green '+' icon in the lower-right corner of the screen.

You can then enter key details for the event that you are creating. Give your event a title and then provide a location. To do this, tap on the map icon and then search for the location in the Google Maps app, which is linked. You can then enter start and end times for the event and set yourself a reminder. Tap on 'View More Options' and you can write a description and assign an icon to signify the event. Once you have finished adding the details, tap 'Save' and your event will be saved to the corresponding date. Tap on the created event to open the details and then tap on the share icon to start sharing the event with other people.

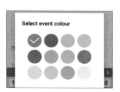

Colour code each new event that you create by tapping on the palette icon next to the title

Add the weather

1 Go to Settings Tap on the More button and then choose the Settings option from the menu.

2 Weather option Now select the 7-day weather forcast option and move the slider on.

3 Weather settings Tap on the Weather Settings option and then tailor the various options.

4 At-a-glance Icons for the next seven days will provide a heads up to the weather.

S Voice

S Voice

Now you can control your Samsung Galaxy device with a range of vocal commands

You'll use it to...

Control apps
Use your voice to interact with apps

Voice dial
Say the number you want to call

Text message
Dictate your text messages

Navigate
Request your directions

Record voice
Store your audio notes for later

Set alarm
Tell your phone when you need to wake up

Fig 1 (right) You can open your apps by simply speaking to the S Voice app

Fig 2 (above) Voice commands trigger a number of services from S Voice

Introducing your personal assistant

S Voice is a voice-command tool; simply use your voice to deliver commands and S Voice will respond. Its capabilities extend to being able to answer general-knowledge questions, as well as acting as a local listing service in order to help find the nearest restaurant, and being able to play music or record memos, among other things.

Ask your device for information

Opening up your Samsung Galaxy device, searching for app icons to tap, waiting for them to open and then finding the right interface and command to issue takes time, and can be inconvenient if you don't have time to spare, or if you have your hands full carrying lots of bags. Maybe you are running to catch a plane, or a disability prevents the easy use of the standard interface. In all of these cases, the S Voice app can prove to be invaluable. It acts like a butler or a maid, hearing your instructions and acting upon them, and if necessary, delivering information based upon those commands. S Voice will perform tasks that might have required a fairly complex command structure, but even basic commands can save time. To perform such commands, open up S

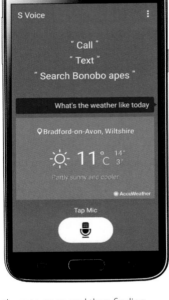

Voice from your App Drawer. If you leave the app for a while then it will move into standby mode. Say "Hi Galaxy" to wake it up. To open YouTube, for example, say "Open YouTube" and the app will then open, in the process presenting the home screen to you.

Control apps by speaking

Yes, you can use S Voice to open up your favourite app, but what if you are already inside the app? There are apps on your Samsung Galaxy that can be controlled by S Voice. For example, you can instruct your device to play a song. S Voice will open the Music Player app and play the track. Once in there, however, you can also tell S Voice to pause the song. You can also tell it to skip to the next track or increase and decrease the volume, in the process providing even more hands-free flexibility.

Activate S Voice

There are different methods of waking up the S Voice system. The most obvious is tapping the app icon, but you can also wake it up from a lock screen. From inside the S Voice Settings menu you can provide a wake-up command that will unlock the phone, but there are other commands that will also start S Voice and then immediately start an app such as Music Player, or open the Camera app or check a schedule. There's one important point you need to remember when enabling the wake-up from lock function: the mic will listen for the commands at all times, which will drain your battery. The easiest way to quickly open the S Voice app is to double-tap the home key. You can activate or disable this feature by going to Settings from the menu icon, but we found that it is the easiest and less cumbersome method of launching this service.

Tap the menu button and then choose 'Example commands' to see what you can say

Set wake-up command

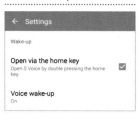

1 Settings Tap the menu icon and choose Settings and then choose Voice wake-up.

2 Set new Ensure the option is turned on and then tap on 'Set wake-up command'.

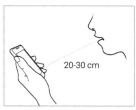

3 Repeat x4 Say the word or phrase four times to enable the app to become familiar with it.

4 Record command With each successful recording, the counter will increase by one. Tap Done.

S Health

S Health

Watch your weight, count steps, check your heartbeat and create a diet plan with S Health

You'll use it to...

Add your details
Cater S Health to you

Compete against yourself
Log and track activities

Keep an eye on your heart
Use your Galaxy's heart rate monitor to get your BPM

Set goals
Challenge yourself and win achievements

Watch your calories
Build a personalised diet

Record your fitness
Log exercise duration and distances

Fig 1 (right) add your details to S Health to get the most out of it

Fig 2 (above) Samsung's latest smart technology is fully utilised in S Health

Fitness on your smartphone

The S Health app has dozens of tools to help you monitor and improve your general health and fitness. At its simplest, S Health can take your basic information (height, weight, age etc) and create a series of customisable goals that are tailored specifically to you. Begin by opening S Health and inputting and saving your details.

Smart fitness

S Health does much more than allow you to log and review all of your fitness and dietary information. With the use of the Galaxy S5, S6 or S7, or a Galaxy Gear (tap the chain icon in the Heart Rate window to sync your smartwatch) you'll be able to keep accurate

information on your exercise, including distance travelled and through the use of GPS the exact route that you took. The first most useful tool that you'll be able to fully utilise with the smartphone or smartwatch is the pedometer. This can be found at the bottom of the main S Health window. Tap the icon then tap pause. From now on, your device will be counting your steps, even when S Health isn't open. The second most useful tool is the heart rate monitor. Again access this from the main window. Once opened press your finger against the monitor on the device (on the S5 this is just below the camera on the back of the phone; the smartwatch will take your pulse from your wrist). After a moment has passed your heart rate will have been taken. If you regularly check your heart rate you can tap on the green chart icon at the bottom-right corner of the heart-rate window to check the fluctuations in your BPM. Tap the Log icon to see a breakdown of all your BPM records.

Watch your steps in S Health

Once you have recorded your steps using the pedometer, tap the chart icon to review your hourly, daily and monthly progress. Tap on the Trophy icon below your calorie count in the pedometer window in order to view the pedometer leader board. Here you can compare your pedometer score with other S Health users. The leader board is split into two categories, Your Rankings and Leader board. The Your Ranking window will show you where you rank in the world against other S Health users. The leader board lets you view and compare yourself against other S Health users.

Setting personal goals

Before you begin recording your exercise and diet it's a good idea to set up some personal goals that you'd like to achieve. Once you've added your details and taken your heart rate tap on the three medals at the top of the main S Health window. Several goals will have been created for you. Tap Set goal on any medal to change the goal parameters. Each goal has different parameters. The step count and calories burnt goals can be logged automatically by S Health. Tap the menu in the top-right corner of the app and tap Food to add details for your Calorie intake goal.

Go to the settings window to change units of measurement for height, weight and distance

Record your exercise

1 **Exercise type** From the Main S Health window tap Exercise. Select the exercise you want.

2 **Set a goal** Tap Set workout goal. Set a goal based on Distance, time or calories burnt. Tap Save.

3 **Start** Begin your work out. To play music, simply tap the play button and get exercising!

4 **Finish Work Out** Once you're done, tap 'Finish' and it shall tell you what you have achieved.

S Health

Fig 3 (above) Watch your calorie intake in S Health

Input your calorie intake

Access all of S Health's tools from the menu button in S Health. In the menu tap on Food. By default the Food page will land on today's date so any info you add will be applied to today. Tap on the date and select a different day on the calendar to back date calorie info. At the top of the Food page you'll see your Calorie intake goal, and how far below or above it you are. Tap the plus icon next to Breakfast, Lunch or Dinner. You'll be taken to an extensive list of food categorised into different types. You can browse by category or use the search tool to find food you've eaten. Most are broken down into a main category, a sub category and the specific food type. Tap on a food type to select it, then input your portion size

More options
Take photos, find your location or sync a smart watch from here

More info
Tap the drop down menu to change the main details of an exercise

Exercise window
This window provides active distance, duration and calorie details

Play music
Play and pause music. Or pre assign music before the exercise

Tap the log icon at the top of a window to view all of your historic fitness information

by adjusting the scale by sliding your finger over it. You can change the measurement of a portion from the drop-down menu. Tap OK when done. Add more food types if need be then tap done at the top of the window. In the next window you can add a time and date of consumption, as well as images and notes. Tap Save and the calorie intake will be added to your food page. Repeat for all meals.

Complete a full workout

Open the main menu and tap Exercise to enter exercise mode. Exercises are split between Running, walking, cycling and hiking. Each exercise has its own preferences but for each one you'll be able to set a workout goal which will be covered in the later tutorial. Tap on the chart icon at the bottom right of the exercise window to review and compare previous exercise sessions. Tap the options icon at the top-right corner of the window and tap Set maximum heart rate. When using a Samsung smartwatch this option will warn you when your heart rate reaches the set maximum heart rate. Once a workout is complete, review the workout's details and add notes and photos as well as share the information via a social network. Workouts will automatically be added to your current goals.

Edit your profile

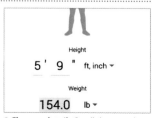

1 Your profile Tap the menu button and select your profile, then tap the three-dot icon and Edit Profile.

2 Change details Scroll down to the section you want to edit and tap the respective item to change it.

Coach tool

1 Create a coach From the main menu tap Coach. Select a topic you want to be coached on.

2 Add information Answer all of the questions that are asked relating to your chosen topic.

Exercise	46
Food	77
Sleep	100
Stress	95

3 Your results Tap on the topic to review your score to determine what to do next.

4 Set a goal Tap Set goal. Select and accept a new goal adding it to the coach page.

S Translator

S Translator

Discover how to use Samsung's simple and accessible translation tool to help you converse and understand your surroundings in foreign countries

You'll use it to...

Converse overseas
Nine different languages are supported

Translate words or phrases
Speak to enter text to be translated

Store translations
Mark translations as favourites to refer back to later

Explore presets
Get quick translations from the database

Hear translations
Listen to audio of your translated text

Fig 1 (right) You can type in text to translate or simply speak it...

Fig 2 (above) The app comes with a range or preset translations across a wide range of categories

Talk to anyone

The S Translator app is a brilliant tool for helping you converse with others and understand what is going on around you in foreign countries. The simple interface makes it quick and easy to translate keywords or complete phrases and keep them safely stored so that you can refer back to them when you need to.

Easy translating

The service supports nine different languages to translate text to and from and you simply select the languages and get typing before tapping on the translate icon. Within

seconds the text will be translated quickly and easily. If you don't fancy typing the text then you can also speak the words or phrases to translate (Fig 1). This is particularly useful for when you need to converse with people in a different language as you can speak words or phrases directly into your device and play the audio of the translated text back to the recipient for a more natural and organic communication process.

Storing phrases

All of the translations that you make can be marked with a star icon. If you then tap the menu icon in the top-left corner of the app you

S Translator

can access a section called Favourites where marked translations that you frequently use will be stored for when you need them the most. Also in the menu is a section called Preset phrases. Tap on this to discover a wide range of words and phrases for your selected language that already come pre-installed in the app (Fig 2). The sort of stuff you'll find here are the most common words and phrases that are on hand to draw on as and when you need to. Finally, exploring the History section is also a good way to revisit previous translations that you may not have marked as favourites.

If you opt to explore the Preset phrases menu then any translated phrases that you are likely to use repeatedly can be stored as favourites by tapping on the star icon next to it, which means they will be added to your own personal Favourites section that you can access easily. And if you change the translation languages then the phrases within the presets section will be changed accordingly. Also, if you delve deeper you will be able to access a variety of different categories, each packed with common translated phrases that apply. Such sections include Business, Directions, Eating and Greetings – everything you need to communicate and get by on your foreign holidays and overseas business trips.

Sound options

As you can ask the app to read aloud the translations for you by tapping the speech icon, you can also explore various options that relate to this function by tapping on the three-dot icon in the top-right corner. Here you can adjust the readout speed (which may help the people you are trying to converse with) and tick the 'Auto read out' box to ensure that everything you type gets spoken to aid the conversational process.

If you need to access older translations quickly, tap the menu icon and choose History

The apps

Start translating

1 Select language 'from' Tap on the language that you wish to translate from and choose one.

2 Select language 'to' Choose the language you would like to translate to and start typing.

3 Make translation When you finish typing, tap on the translate icon and the text will appear.

4 Mark it Tap the star to favourite the translation so you can access it quickly from your Favourites.

Facebook

Facebook remains the premier social-media client available to all Samsung Galaxy users

You'll use it to...

Chat
Talk to your friends and family

Browse timelines
See what people have been up to

Meet new people
Find and add new friends

Post statuses
Tell people about your day

Share photos
Add photos and videos to your timeline

Fig 1 (right) Scroll through recent content added by friends and family

Fig 2 (above) Add a new status or share pictures on your timeline easily

Stay in touch using Facebook

Facebook is the ultimate social-media client for Samsung Galaxy users who want to chat to their friends and family. Galaxy owners can use the chat function to keep in contact with their friends and even start video chats using their smartphone's front-facing camera. The official Facebook app also supports group chat.

Manage your Facebook timeline

The timeline feature within the Facebook app is the hub for all Samsung Galaxy users. It provides each person with a place to post their status

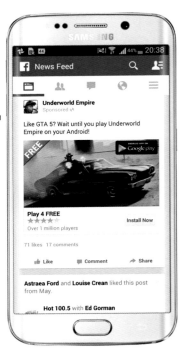

details and stores them in chronological order. But dig a little deeper and your timeline can be so much more. Samsung Galaxy users can choose to add details about themselves to their own timeline, and even set individual privacy settings to stop or allow certain people from viewing the content they hold. Each user can then set a profile picture to represent them and a cover photo to appear at the top. Once you've started connecting with new people through the Facebook app, you'll find that posts from them appear on your timeline. These posts are fully interactive and users can choose to like them, or simply respond to them by posting a comment. In some cases you may want to delete the post, but this is easily done by pressing the small arrow at the top-right of the post and then selecting the Delete option. Samsung Galaxy users can also explore their friend's timeline by selecting their name from the Friends list. You'll be able to see their personal status, images they've linked with their account and posts created by others.

Manage media on your account

As well as being a great place for posting statuses and chatting with friends, Facebook has a comprehensive suite of features for those who want to share and embed media files on their timelines. While posting a status, users can attach photos to it, as well as designate these photos to a specific album. It's also possible to load any number of photos to your account and create a virtual library of them. Similarly, users can record and upload videos to their account, which automatically embed themselves on to the timeline for other people to watch and enjoy.

Take control of app settings

Samsung Galaxy users have a plethora of settings waiting for them in the Facebook app. The most important ones link to your privacy and how much of your posted content you want others to see. You can set restraints on some content, or even make individual posts available to people outside of your friends. Dig a little deeper and you'll find settings that enable you to block specific users from seeing content and even look through sync options to automatically add photos and videos to your Facebook account.

Change the Refresh Interval option within App Settings to help preserve battery life

Start chatting to friends

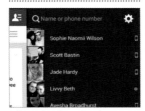

1 Start chat Press the chat icon at the top-right of your screen and select a person to start chatting.

2 Messaging Not only can you type messages to your contact, you can add emoticons as well.

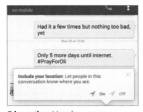

3 Location Use the message bubble to decide if you want to share your location with them.

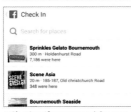

4 Sharing If you tapped On, you can choose your location from the menu that appears.

Twitter

Follow trends, meet new people and post your own views all within the Twitter app

You'll use it to...

Follow people
Follow friends, families and celebrities

Tweet
Post your own thoughts and opinions

Send messages
Send private messages to people

Share posts
Retweet your favourite posts

Sync accounts
Merge Twitter accounts together

Enjoy videos
Watch video in Twitter's integrated player

Fig 1 (right) Read through the tweets from people you follow in one menu

Fig 2 (above) You can add photos and locations to tweets with ease

Enjoy Twitter wherever you are

Twitter is a social media client, where users can create snippets of their thoughts and post them to the world. Although there are several Twitter apps currently available for Galaxy, the official Twitter app remains the best choice. The app is split into menus, enabling you to find your profile, news feed and your private messages.

Tweeting directly from your Galaxy

At the heart of Twitter is the act of sending out tweets. These are small posts that are linked to your profile and can be started by tapping the What's Happening? field at the bottom of the screen. There are no real rules to what you can post, apart from each one must be 140 characters or less; so don't expect the chance to write any in-depth posts here. At the bottom of the tweet box, you'll also find the option to add a video or image to the tweet, so other people can watch it and share it on their profiles for their followers to interact with. Your created tweets are then sent to all the people that follow you, who can then interact with it and you can interact with their tweets too. As well as simply reading each other's tweets, you can also retweet it on to your own page, write a reply or favourite it. Whenever you create a tweet, you can also direct it to a specific person by starting the tweet with the @ symbol and then their username. Just remember that although your tweet is meant for one person, everyone will be able to see it. You'll want to consider direct messaging if it's an important or private message that you want to send.

Sending private messages

By pressing the envelope icon found on your profile, you'll be taken to the Direct Messages section. Here you can find all of the private messages that were sent to you, but aren't publicly available for others to see. To reply to a message just press on one and begin typing away. Again, it's important to remember that you can only use 140 characters or less. When a new direct message is sent to you, a small notification will appear at the top of your profile and by pressing on that, you'll be taken directly to it to read and reply.

Discover even more on your Galaxy device

The Discover section on the Twitter app is where you'll want to go to find out what everyone is talking about. It contains the most trending topics at that time and by simply pressing on one of them, you can see tweets dedicated to it. Scroll down a bit further and you can see how the people you follow are interacting with the trends, or even see the tweets they have recently favourited. Right at the bottom of the Discover section, you'll find people that you've been recommended to follow. These recommendations tend to be based on people who share the same interests as you. Simply tap the icon next to their name to follow.

You can find the highlights Twitter thinks you'll like by tapping the three dots then Highlights

Add media & location

1 Tweeting From your news feed, press on the white box at the bottom of the page to tweet.

2 Options After typing out the tweet, you can now use the media and location add-ons.

3 Photos Choose the camera icon to upload an image from your device or a cloud account.

4 Location Press the location marker to add a map and marker of your current location.

The next-gen tech magazine for all forward-thinkers

Hands on testing
More than just purchasing advice, Gadget explains how the hottest kit works and brings you practical advice

The latest tech
Featuring all of the most exciting tech, including drones, 3D printers, wearables and VR

Plus cool competitions!

About the mag

ubscribers to...

Gadget

Try 3 issues for £5 in the UK*
or just $5.92 per issue in the USA**
(saving 53% off the newsstand price)

For amazing offers please visit
www.imaginesubs.co.uk/gadget

Quote code ZGGZINE
Or telephone UK 0844 249 0270+ Overseas +44 (0) 1795 418 676
+Calls will cost 7p per minute plus your telephone company's access charge